BREAKING THE CHAINS

BREAKING THE CHAINS

Collective action for social justice among the rural poor of Bangladesh

BOSSE KRAMSJO and
GEOFFREY D. WOOD

with a Foreword by FARUQUE AHMED

Practical Action Publishing Ltd
25 Albert Street, Rugby, CV21 2SD, Warwickshire, UK
www.practicalactionpublishing.com

© Intermediate Technology Publications Ltd, 1992

First published 1992\Digitised 2008

ISBN 10: 1 85339 024 0
ISBN 13 Paperback: 9781853390241
ISBN Library Ebook: 9781780444581
Book DOI: https://doi.org/10.3362/9781780444581

All rights reserved. No part of this publication may be reprinted or reproduced or utilized in any form or by any electronic, mechanical, or other means, now known or hereafter invented, including photocopying and recording, or in any information storage or retrieval system, without the written permission of the publishers.

A catalogue record for this book is available from the British Library.

The authors, contributors and/or editors have asserted their rights under the Copyright Designs and Patents Act 1988 to be identified as authors of their respective contributions.

Since 1974, Practical Action Publishing has published and disseminated books and information in support of international development work throughout the world. Practical Action Publishing is a trading name of Practical Action Publishing Ltd (Company Reg. No. 01159018), the wholly owned publishing company of Practical Action. Practical Action Publishing trades only in support of its parent charity objectives and any profits are covenanted back to Practical Action (Charity Reg. No. 247257, Group VAT Registration No. 880 9924 76).

Typeset by Inforum, Rowlands Castle, Hants, UK

Reasonable efforts have been made to publish reliable data and information, but the author and publisher cannot assume responsibility for the validity of all materials or for the consequences of their use.

The manufacturer's authorised representative in the EU for product safety is Lightning Source France, 1 Av. Johannes Gutenberg, 78310 Maurepas, France. compliance@lightningsource.fr

Contents

FOREWORD *by Faruque Ahmed*	vi
PREFACE	vii
GLOSSARY	viii
PART ONE: INTRODUCTION *by Geoffrey D. Wood*	1
PART TWO: CASE STUDIES *by Bosse Kramsjo*	35
Greater solidarity for greater power	37

Fights for legal control of khas resources
    Khas ponds; Housing; Rice paddies; A marsh;
    A deep tubewell; Vested land
	41

Resistance to exploitation by the rich
    Village touts; False claims for religious purposes;
    A fraudulent sharecropper
	62

Women fight for their rights
    The life of Amena Begum from misery to dignity;
    Women against divorce; An unregistered marriage;
    Dignity and dowry; Literacy
	70

Increasing wages and incomes
    Food for work; The daily wage;
    Equal pay for equal work
	82

Income generation	91
Popular theatre for mobilization	95
Organizational strength for greater power – *the way forward*	100

Foreword

The poor in Bangladesh are in chains. Though invisible, the chains are powerful and have kept millions of people prisoners of poverty. What are these chains and how can the poor break these chains? To develop an understanding of these chains and provide support to the poor to enable them to break the chains has been at the core of Proshika's Participatory Development Strategy. The unshackling of the chains calls for empowerment of the poor. It is a process of organization-building among the poor, heightening their consciousness about the forces of underdevelopment, developing their material autonomy and increasing their participation so that they assume more control of their life and livelihood. This process of empowerment has enabled people to take social, economic and cultural action for their development. Some examples of these actions are documented as case studies from Proshika's Area Development Centres (ADCs) by Mr Bosse Kramsjo who spent a number of years in Bangladesh as a volunteer from Swallows of Sweden. He documented these case studies to show a different image of Bangladesh. The prevalent image of Bangladesh in Western countries, through the aegis of the media, has been an image of disaster, population boom and poverty, where few initiatives are taken by the people to overcome their poverty. The case studies show that people are capable of taking great initiatives for their development.

The introduction to the case studies is written by Dr Geoffrey D. Wood, Director of the Centre for Development Studies, University of Bath who has also spent many years in Bangladesh doing poverty-focused research, and his writings are quite outstanding in terms of their depth and breadth of analysis. The introduction provides the analysis of the socio-economic and political context of Bangladesh in which the collective action of the poor, as documented by Mr Kramsjo, take place.

I hope *Breaking the Chains* can serve as a resource book for development workers, researchers and policy makers.

QAZI FARUQUE AHMED
Executive Director
Proshika
January 1992

Preface

I had the privilege of moving around freely within the Proshika areas of work for almost a year and a half and workers and organized group members always showed great interest and patience, although discussions or inquiries often lasted well beyond midnight and travelling to meetings sometimes was difficult for some of them. I learned a lot through the innumerable meetings with organized groups and discussions with field workers, for which I am very grateful.

Faruque-bhai and all of the Proshika central staff always had five minutes to spare which often became an hour or so. Our discussions were very open-minded, fruitful and often mixed with some good stories. I thank them for many a good time and for important talks over development issues and the mobilization of the rural poor.

These case studies were collected over three months at the beginning of 1986. They are the result of the efforts of the organized villagers whose stories we heard. The Proshika field workers were very helpful and without the co-operation of Asad-bhai and Harun-bhai, this volume would not have been possible.

Finally, thanks to Alasdair and Vicki, who took the time to improve the language.

BOSSE KRAMSJO
Lecturer in Development Studies

Glossary

acre	100 decimals = 0.4 hectares
ADC	Area Development Centre, Proshika Office
BADC	Bangladesh Agricultural Development Corporation
bangsho	lineage
BARD	Bangladesh Academy for Rural Development (formerly the Academy for Rural Development)
bari	kin groups
bheel	open water bodies
bideshi	foreigners
bigha	0.134 hectares (1 hectare = 7.47 bighas = 2/47 acres)
boro	winter season paddy crop
BRDB	Bangladesh Rural Development Board
CARE	Co-operative American Relief Everywhere
CIDA	Canadian International Development Agency
Circle Officer	Senior official of *thana*, now replaced by UNO
CUSO	Canadian University Service Overseas
DTW	Deep Tube Well
foot	0.305m
godown	warehouse
gherao	non-violent occupation of, for example, government office
billa	marriage
HYV	high-yielding variety (of rice)
IDRP	Integrated Rural Development Programme
IRRI	International Rice Research Institute; high-yielding varieties of rice developed by IRRI.
khas	government-owned land and ponds (strictly untitled land)
kurmi	worker, Proshika fieldworker
lakh	100 000
LGRDC	Ministry of Local Government, Rural Development Board
LLP	Low Lift Pump
mahajan	money-lender
matbar	headman of a village, social leader
maund	approx. 37kg
mile	1.609km
NGO	non-government organization
para	part of a village, a neighbourhood within a village
paribar	nuclear households
puja	festival
pucca	solid
RLF	Revolving Loan Fund
samity	society, organized group
seer	0.933kg
shalish	village court for arbitration
taka	US$1 = 30 taka, £1 = 65 taka
thana	a police station; unit of local administration, containing 6-8 unions
union	smallest administrative unit, 4400 in the country
UNO	*Upazila nirbahi* Officer, administrative head of an *upazila*
upazila	sub-district, 462 in the country;
zamindar	landlord (strictly a collector of revenue)

PART I: INTRODUCTION

During the 1980s Bangladesh became an international laboratory for poverty studies and experiments to overcome poverty. Unique historical circumstances following from the partition of India at independence in 1947, through to the break-up of Pakistan in 1971, left East Bengal to face the remaining years of the seventies and beyond with a rapidly growing population, a fragile farming system, rising landlessness, few capital resources, degraded infrastructure, a decimated intelligentsia, a relatively uniform yet precarious ecology arising from deltaic topography, the absence of a democratic tradition with an over-reliance upon the military and bureaucracy to secure policy and political objectives, and an overwhelming dependency upon foreign aid and technical assistance.

Bangladesh was, in fact, one of the poorest countries in the world. The dominant role of donors ensured that foreigners (*bideshis*) were extensively involved in making studies of poverty in the country, working closely with concerned (surviving) members of the educated classes. I would like to think that I made a contribution in this respect through the publication of *Exploitation and the Rural Poor* based on collaborative research at the Bangladesh Academy for Rural Development (BARD), Comilla during 1974–6. This was one of the first publications to draw attention to the problems of class and poverty, and to the problem of landlessness, now very familiar issues. Foreign agencies became extensively involved in the education and training of a new generation of Bangladeshis throughout government and academic institutions, to the point where foreign technical assistance now performs more of an aid-policing than technical-input role. However, with continuing aid dependency, the significant presence of foreign 'experts' has internationalized the poverty problems of Bangladesh as well as encouraged its laboratory status.

A key ingredient in the growing awareness of poverty in the country has been the emergence of non-government organizations (NGOs). Although there are several hundred of these bodies loosely concerned with development, a few stand out as having made a significant contribution both to an understanding of the poverty process and to the development of strategies to remove it. These NGOs have drawn upon an important indigenous tradition of creative and independent thinking which was never suppressed, either during the Pakistan era or during the subsequent donor raj. Indeed, before considering these NGOs, the role of government should not be dismissed entirely, despite the popularity of knocking officialdom, since elements within the government have always shared in this creative and constructive tradition.

Limitations of official strategy for rural development

The most relevant government body in this respect was the Academy for Rural Development at Comilla, which after Liberation became known as the Bangladesh Academy for Rural Development (BARD). This institution pioneered rural development experiments in the Indian sub-continent during the 1960s, and in so doing acquired a considerable international reputation. Based upon the socio-economic profile for the Comilla region, the country was conceived of as a society of smallholding farmers (though actually it was a peasant economy) whose fortunes would be enhanced through credit- and input-cooperatives and, later co-operation around Deep Tube-Well (DTW) and Low Lift Pump (LLP) irrigation technologies in order to grow dry-season high-yielding varieties of rice (HYVs). This was an action-research strategy, in which professional staff at the academy inaugurated a co-operative system at village and sub-district levels, and then studied the various technical and organizational aspects of their innovations. The programme spread through the Comilla district in the 1960s, attracting much attention as a universal model (the two-tier system) for East Bengal as well as providing useful insights applicable elsewhere. By the end of the decade, the decision had already been taken to replicate the model as the Integrated Rural Development Programme (IRDP) for the whole of East Bengal. After Liberation, this strategy was resurrected, and in 1981 achieved permanent status within the Ministry of Local Government, Rural Development and Co-operatives (LGRDC) as the Bangladesh Rural Development Board (BRDB). The network of village-level co-operatives (*Krishi Samabaya Samity*

KSS) and sub-district federations (*Upazila* Central Co-operative Associations UCCA) remains.

The model had two major problems however. First, the socio-economic profile around Comilla was not as typical for East Bengal as first assumed; other parts of the country were characterized by more obvious class inequalities, with larger numbers of peasants-cum-landlords, a greater incidence of sharecropping and a much higher proportion of landless labourers. Second, even in the Comilla region of small farmers, less sharecropping and less landlessness, it was clear, from both pre-Liberation in-house reviews and our post-Liberation findings for *Exploitation and the Rural Poor*, that significant inequalities and conflict existed, reinforced to some extent by the introduction of the co-operative system. The KSS were being captured by village élites and deployed in their own narrow interests. The image of smallholding farmers with a propensity to consensual decision making and collective action for mutual benefit could not be sustained.

Despite these limitations, however, the principle of action-research and a style of local analysis and problem-solving had been established. Unfortunately, both the academy and the government sought to replicate the model rather than the style. These arguments were acknowledged by progressive and thoughtful officials within government, notably the secretary for LGRDC in the mid-1970s, and later for Agriculture, A.Z.M. Obaidullah Khan. In the late 1970s, he sponsored a USAID-funded study, 'The Land Occupancy Survey', which revealed perhaps for the first time the variations in landholding patterns across the country and indicated the empirical limitations of the Comilla socio-economic profile as a relevant description for the country as a whole. If the KSS were showing weaknesses even within their region of introduction, they were unlikely to meet the needs of the poor (whether small owners, sharecroppers or landless labourers, and, significantly, women) elsewhere in the country where there were even less socially hospitable conditions. With the momentum behind the extension of the co-operative model too strong to resist (reinforced by the drafting into central government of ex-Academy staff after Liberation and the legacy of the Comilla experiment as a rural development totem), the mantle of poverty-focused creative analysis and institutional innovation shifted away from government towards the recently emerging NGOs. It is as if the style of Comilla was passed on without the model. The challenge for today's NGOs is to avoid the same mistake, namely the routinization of innovative style.

Conditions for emergence of development NGOs

The emergence of the early development NGOs in Bangladesh was not just a reflection of this gap in analysis and policy, or even primarily of the growing awareness among concerned Bangladeshi observers about the dimensions of poverty. The political conditions in the aftermath of Liberation were crucial. The Awami League, as the nationalist party of Bengali independence, inherited political office but rapidly abused its mandate in an orgy of incompetence and corruption. From the beginning of 1975, it engaged in the wholesale repression of political opposition, especially that of the Marxist left, organized in various regional groupings, as it attempted to establish a one-party state under presidential rule. The coup in August 1975, followed by the sequence of coups in November 1975, brought the army under Zia Rahman to power, and continued the repression of the left both within the military and outside it. With the domination of the army continuing more or less unbroken until December 1990, the opportunity for political parties openly to espouse the interests of the poor against the vested interests of those dominating the state was severely restricted. At best, a benevolent dictatorship could be hoped for, which would, of course, be more accountable to foreign donors than to progressive internal opinion. The more imaginative development NGOs, however, played an increasingly crucial role in this delicate political equation.

Their origins, from the mid-1970s, arose from a combination of the resistance to repression of formal, radical and progressive politics; a generation of young activists with political values and courage shaped by their experiences during the struggle for liberation from Pakistani domination; and the availability of donor support. It is also true that some were set up by expatriate Bangladeshis returning in the later 1970s from succcessful professional activities abroad (for example, accountancy and academia). The main impetus, however, reflected a concerned generation of students, active on the university campuses in the late 1960s against Pakistan's domination, active during the liberation war itself, both within refugee camps in India as well as underground within East Bengal, and active in the immediate aftermath of the war in various emergency relief campaigns, often involving foreign charities and voluntary organizations. Without the opportunity to translate these immediate concerns into a longer-term political commitment, alongside their witnessing of the criminal neglect of the poor by the state, this generation of young Bangladeshis turned to the voluntary, and eventually funded, NGO sector as the outlet for their frustrated ambitions on behalf of the poor in their newly liberated country.

Proshika's agrarian analysis

I was privileged to come into early contact with these groups, and one in particular, Proshika. My assistant during the research at BARD, Comilla was Mohamed Yahiya. After my departure at the end of 1975, he joined Proshika there. This organization had started in 1975 as a project of the Canadian University Service Overseas (CUSO), and became a separate Bangladeshi organization in the following year with two branches, one in Dhaka and one in Comilla, supported by core funding from the Canadian International Development Agency (CIDA), and continuing inputs from CUSO, until the early 1980s. CIDA continues to support the two, now separate, organizations of Proshika. Md. Yahiya introduced me to the two branches in 1978 on a return visit, and eventually I worked most closely with the Dhaka wing, now Proshika Manobik Unnayan Kendra (henceforth referred to here as Proshika). This introduction will conclude with a longer description of Proshika's approaches to development work among the poor; here, the remarks are confined to its view of the problems which the poor face. The basis of our initial association was the analysis contained in *Exploitation and the Rural Poor* and the recognition that few development agencies (academic, donor and government) really understood the scale of landlessness as the root cause of pervasive poverty and remained locked into trickle-down strategies by concentrating upon the economic development of farmers through enhanced agricultural technologies embodied in the Green Revolution. Few also understood or appreciated the social processes through which landlessness arose and poverty was reproduced in the rural political economy, or that the state was not benign in these circumstances. There was a strong sense that to work with the poor through ideas of empowerment and conscientization was subversive; some of our early discussions were distinctly clandestine in a way which now appears unnecessary.

The basic ideology as it emerged over time among the initial leadership in Proshika was that class subordination for landless women and men was experienced more as individual rather than collective exploitation. The rural political economy consisted of class relations expressed through patron–client structured hierarchies, with poor landowners, sharecropping tenants and landless labourers constituting a class of clients tied individually to patrons who might be landlords, moneylenders or employers, usually in combination. The poor rural peasantry in Bangladesh thus exemplified the familiar Marxian problem of a class in itself needing to become a class for itself as a precondition for its own effective action. Original Marxists, up to and including Trotsky, dismissed the capacity of the peasantry to move itself from one condition to the other; the jump from individual perceptions of injustice to collective action to rectify that injustice was considered too great, and certainly required leadership external to the peasantry.

The Bolshevik Revolution was premised upon this assumption. Eric Wolf in *Peasant Wars of the Twentieth Century* also pointed to the difficulty for the peasant in moving from a passive recognition of wrongs to implementing the means for setting them right. He listed a number of issues: the isolation of rural work – working as scattered individuals in distant fields; the tyranny of work – long hours dictated by seasonal imperatives; the competition among the poor for scarce land resources to rent, or for security of employment by accepting tied conditions; the inability to attend meetings and rallies because of work obligations and financial constraints; the problem of communication in a non-literate world; and the absence of control over or access to the means of communication.

To these we may add a lack of empathy for other poor outside localized experiences of exploitation and oppression; a loyalty to a familiar individualized survival option involving the acceptance of subordinate status; the fragmentation or disarticulation of potential class solidarity on horizontal lines through incorporation into vertically aligned, factional groups led by leaders of one's lineage (*bangsho*); and, under such structural conditions, the untested unity of one's own class to deliver a substitute survival package, sustained over a long time period. I have always been impressed by an encounter in my Comilla fieldwork with a poor, marginal farmer who was obliged to sell his labour. He was about 35 years old. He recounted in great detail how he and others like him in his *para* (a distinct grouping of households in a village, often tracing common genealogical descent) were being dominated and exploited through low wages, high rents, exorbitant interest rates and the manipulation of opportunities for scarce employment by Abdul Ghafor, the largest landholder, businessman, dealer and tout (a Bangla expression to denote a corrupt broker with official connections, especially with government) in the *para*. When I asked him what was the furthest distance he had travelled in his life, he replied with a review of other villages visited. When we identified them on my map, the answer was eight miles.

Converting affliction into action

This underlies a distinction made in academic circles between protest and revolution. The term 'revolution', especially in South Asia, conjures up an image of Marxist-inspired armed movements fighting official armies over sustained periods of time with the support, active or passive, of the peasantry. The term therefore induces fear of immediate threat to the interests of the middle classes (commercial, professional and official), which then endorse repressive state action and a widespread application of sedition laws. NGOs in Bangladesh have, therefore, been at pains to describe themselves and their objectives in other terms. If, however, we adopt a more generic use of the term revolution to refer to processes of structural transformation in the society, without assuming violent upheaval as a prerequisite, then the distinction between revolution and protest remains highly significant to the whole question of extending the horizons of the poor beyond eight miles, together with a corresponding sense of opportunity.

The south Asian region is replete with examples of protest activity among the rural poor. Colonial officers were always dealing with 'agrarian discontent', particularly at harvest times with struggles over crop shares. Such activity reflects an acute awareness of local, immediate injustices involving intense hostility to those held directly responsible, whether landlords or officials. The personalities are known, the hostility is not abstract. Typically such protest was shortlived, with single-issue objectives which, if achieved, led no further. Often, the fear of the ruling classes that such protest would spread resulted in quick and comprehensive repression deploying the forces of the local state or their own retainers. Indeed, the anticipation of such immediate counter-repression played a major part in maintaining the quiescence of the poor; apathy is less a state of mind than a rational calculation of the odds.

Thus a large jump in perception and calculation is required to translate discontent into a sense of class and a programme of action leading to structural transformation. The problem, then, is not the awareness among the poor of their exploited condition, but the degree of sophistication in that awareness together with the objective capacity to act on it. I have always been worried by the inference that the poor need to be taught either how poor they are or the immediate explanations for their plight. Poor peasants who have lost land recently through their inability to repay usurious loans basically know the score. We must also accept that such people have kin with similar experiences in their own and nearby villages. And we must also accept that rural-rural migration is long established in Bangladesh and has provided an opportunity for broadening class perceptions. More recently, urban and external migration have added to this.

But the pressures which fragment and individualize the experience of exploitation persist. The family remains the unit of primary reference, in which ultimate responsibility for ensuring survival or enhancement resides. There has to be a strong sense in which Banfield's thesis of 'amoral familism' applies (Banfield 1958): behaviour within the family is bound by moral ties; behaviour outside the family can be structured within concentric circles through which action is increasingly instrumental. But since the poor family as a unit is vulnerable when acting in isolation from others, there is a strategic imperative to extend the sense of moral community outwards through some of those concentric circles, to include others in similar positions, for example. Conscientization reminds people of their vulnerability as individuals or families, and encourages the notion that strength lies in unity with other families similarly placed. It is the gaining of this strength which constitutes the revolution for the poor in Bangladesh; how precisely this strength is to be used is a secondary question. Revolution in the rhetorical sense of 'armed mass movements advancing upon the edifices of the state and those classes protected by such edifices' is only one option for the use of that strength. The first step towards gaining strength is the one described in this volume, namely 'breaking the chains'.

Several issues arise at this point. What are the chains to be broken? Are they the same for all the poor? In other words, are the poor homogeneous? Can poor people break their own chains or do they require external assistance? What are the consequences of relying on such assistance? What prevents chains being reimposed, or new ones binding? To remove chains implies the gaining of freedom, the establishment of meaningful, universal human rights of citizenship, that is, the right to participate in the political process and equality before the law, accountable government and unlocked prices in market transactions. In Bangladesh, the acquisition of freedom, so defined, would be the revolution, to be distinguished from locally resolved protest (whether through concession or repression), implying no structural transformation in the relation between rich and poor, and to be distinguished from guns on the parapet.

In most societies, the chains would be characterized by class and gender overlaid by the subtle processes of legitimizing ideologies. To a considerable extent this holds true for Bangladesh, but kin norms and religion have to be added as key dimensions of ideology and culture. There are always dangers in [Western] outsiders referring critically to the function of religion in other societies; but it is a nettle that has to be grasped. Let us, however, return to religion later, after first considering class and gender.

Class chains

Some anthropologists would criticize the use of class as an appropriate concept in the analysis of rural Bangladesh, seeing it as an analytical import from the industrialized capitalist West. They have pointed to the significance of demographic rather than social differentiation between rural families at different points in their respective life cycles; to the significance of patron–client dyads in the formation of rural solidarities; to the importance of *bangshos* as immediate points of reference beyond the family in which families of differing economic status are bound together through ties of brotherhood, albeit vertically aligned in terms of wealth. But as long as we do not insist upon consciousness as a necessary element in the existence of class, then we are certainly observing the systematic relations of exploitation between significant owners of the means of production and those separated from such ownership.

In rural Bangladesh, to own land or other assets beyond the utility of one's own family labour supply places that family in a powerful position over other families whose productive assets fail to absorb their own labour supply. Those with surplus land and assets assert control over others: via quasi-monopolistic employment in a labour surplus economy; via usurious moneylending in a credit-, capital- and welfare-scarce economy; via the control over the allocation of land for tenancy production; and via the prices set for rents. That these forms of control may be exercised through multiplex patron–client relationships, within localized vertical hierarchies, often reinforced by kin loyalties, does not undermine the validity of seeing such relationships in systematic class terms.

These patterns of domination extend beyond the scope of one's own immediate means of production to the control of access to other opportunities in the locality, especially those available through officialdom, but also to those existing within quasi-market structures. Patronage has been extended into non-agricultural spheres, though elements of reciprocity between patron and client have been lost in the process. Access to employment on a local rural works scheme, for example, may depend not only upon the applicant being poor, but upon favoured client status within patronage networks through which the work is allocated, that is not by virtue of right but through a connection for which the price is continued subservience. Similar evidence emerges from the implementation of the government's Rural Poor Programme, which I examined in the late 1980s. This involves the formation of landless groups (both women and men) for credit and savings purposes, and provides for some entitlement to services in support of income-generating activities. The official of the BRDB, responsible for the programme in the locality, is most likely to approach the heads of the strong families in the village, that is, the key patrons, for assistance. These patrons will then nominate the membership of such groups, and may even charge commission along with the official. Sometimes the groups may be fictitious, in the sense that the members are never told of their new status, but the formal existence of such a group may release funds for the excavation of a pond within a patron's control. From these examples we can understand that a crucial element in the exercise of power, especially under conditions of development resource flows, is the domination of information. Ignorance is always a chain, but this ignorance is the outcome of a class-structured alliance between the state, through its officials, and dominant classes in the locality.

The notion of class is complicated in other ways in rural Bangladesh. The significance of landlessness cannot of course be underestimated in a society where the population is 90 per cent rural, more than half of which is effectively without land while the remainder relies heavily upon the use of its own family labour for most operations, except during intensive transplanting and harvesting periods. Furthermore, the overall conditions for the country in the global economy do not offer much prospect for export-led employment generation, and domestic markets remain constrained by this vicious circle of low-level effective demand. Clearly, these conditions have prompted efforts towards targeting the landless for income-generation programmes within the countryside, though not necessarily connected with agriculture, a factor which has been a weakness of some of these strategies. (The prospects for linking empowerment and employment opportunities directly to agriculture are discussed below.)

When we turn to the social forms of action and consciousness, however, then we have to question the utility of the 'landlessness' label as a target for mobilization efforts or for the delivery of income-generation services. Within the *para* of a village, nuclear households (*paribar*) are arranged into extended kin groups (*bari*), and according to circumstances there will be varying degrees of co-operation and solidarity between them. A landless *paribar* may be part of a closely knit kin group of otherwise non-landless *paribar*. Is this landless *paribar* to be extracted from this unit of solidarity and encouraged to participate in another, involving *paribar* in the outer concentric circles of moral attribution simply on the basis of the single criterion of landlessness?

Alongside this practical complication of social class definition for action purposes, whether in the sense of delivery or mobilization, there is another. These agrarian communities are dynamic, not static, in structure. Landlessness is a process; yesterday's small farmer is today's landless, today's small farmer is tomorrow's landless.

Within the *bari*, between them, and between *para*, the inevitability of this process is known. To the outsider, the distinction between a landless family and a smallholding one may be highly significant, enabling a crude reading-off of primary reference group, political allegiance and needs from the single criterion of ownership of the means of production. The distinction may also be necessary to a concerned donor or NGO, regardless of its social artificiality, in order to justify the flows of scarce funds to the poorest of the poor. Such a distinction makes very little sense to insiders, and certainly cannot be used as an indicator of behavioural propensity. Such targeting on the basis of crude notions of class may be convenient for poverty-focused delivery strategies, but it can never be a guide to mobilization and the breaking of chains. Indeed, the precarious smallholder may remain more 'enchained' than his landless kinsman, who has been 'liberated' into destitution, stripped of collateral and no longer even qualifying for certain forms of exploitation (such as usurious loans, or deteriorating tenancy conditions).

We can conclude that class relations feature strongly in the chains, but we have to be wary of simple income or asset criteria as a basis for classification, especially when either trying to understand the circumstances of spontaneous social action or mobilizing for action. Failure to be sophisticated in one's analysis at this point can lead to misconceptions about natural units of solidarity, and over-optimism about the extent of mutual trust in small groups, as well about substituting horizontal (class) loyalties for vertical (kin or lineage) ones. By the same token, crude classification can lead to an under-estimation of the potential within communities for landless, marginal and small farmers to engage in genuinely collective action. The need for this caution cannot be overstated if social action is to be extended beyond the phase of protest into sustained behaviour with structural implications for changing the balance of political power.

Gender chains

The chains are also about gender relations. As the academic literature on women in poor countries grows, so it does in Bangladesh, and professional males concerned with development become daily more aware of the significantly different sets of chains which confine all women, but especially the poor. It has been interesting to observe over the last two decades in Bangladesh how prominent women have been in struggles at all levels of society, despite that society being typified by many outsiders as among the worst examples of female oppression. There is an apparent paradox between the view which dwells upon female subordination and the evidence of female social action. While not wishing to deny the systematic disadvantages which face women, especially rural and poor, this paradox arises from the way the initial questions are asked about women. Much commentary proceeds from the question 'How are women constrained?' instead of asking 'What do women do?' The first treats women, *a priori*, as passive (intransitive); the second as active (transitive). *Breaking the Chains* is about action. It is concerned with the second question rather than the first.

Nevertheless the structural position for most women in Bangladesh determines particular cultural forms for the female exercise of power, and establishes the consequences for women who move out of these cultural norms. When men break chains, they can do so in a way which is consistent with the gender norms about men even though they will be confronting other cultural rules about deference; that is, within kin and lineage hierarchies; perhaps against elders; the undermining of traditional norms of respect for educated, professional and officer classes; and of course religion. Indeed, in a certain sense, successfully struggling men are displaying a virility and may earn on this dimension the grudging respect of their opponents. Such behaviour can be seen as confirming an aspect of masculinity, namely an aggressive stance in the public sphere. Not so for women in a society where the cultural norms, policed by men and acculturated women in the interests of men, define femininity *inter alia* as quiescent, supplicant nest-building and caring for family members.

Women do exercise power within this definition, and the significance of this power needs to be acknowledged. Sarah White's (1992) study in Rajshahi was counter-intuitive in this sense, exploring and identifying arenas of power for women where none had been assumed previously by studies written from a Western feminist perspective. Her basic argument is that while the patriarchal thesis draws heavily upon a distinction between public and private spheres in the observation of gender behaviour, we cannot assume that the physical location of behaviour is indicative of who exercises power within these locations. Since we have always known that males participate in the decisions and the allocation of work and resources in the private sphere where some women only reside, should we assume that men are the only ones to participate in the public sphere simply because women do not reside there? In addition to their labour and management responsibilities within the private, family sphere which is the source of much *de facto* power, women who venture out of the homestead only in *purdah* nevertheless engage in market behaviour. They do so both directly, through trading in minor livestock, barter and credit to neighbouring families, but indirectly, and importantly, through decisions over land use, buying and selling of land and major livestock, landleasing strategies, government or private loan options, trading produce, investment in business or agriculture, and so on.

However, even with this argument, White would acknowledge that a woman can exercise such power only by remaining apparently within the cultural norms of femininity, acting out the patriarchal rules, playing the game. The power cannot be seen to be hers. This proposition raises at least three issues of interpretation:

o Is this 'acting out' consciously instrumental behaviour by women who have broken the chains in their own minds but are not yet sufficiently confident of success to do so publicly? Many women in many societies are forced into hypocritical behaviour of this kind, deliberately stroking the collective ego of the male community rather than risking open confrontation.

o Are the patriarchal rules so internalized, are women so acculturated, that no other route to power can offer itself within the realms of normative possibility? Some might argue that such adherence to a dependent exercise of power is indicative of false consciousness, but surely this is a proposition which can be asked only of one culture by another outside it?

o Can we accept that women's conformity to these cultural norms of femininity is as much functional to them as constraining. That is to say, their lives are organized, albeit within a framework of apparent dominant male interest, as a reflection of key imperatives in the biological, labour and social reproduction of society in which the management of female sexuality is central, is consequently highly valued, and is consequently acutely insecure and requires physical and cultural rules of protection to avoid the prospect of greater female violation.

These questions can only be resolved empirically, and are posed here to distinguish between women in different situations, with varying sets of objective conditions and related subjective perceptions. The key principle to understanding the character of gender chains is that the cultural norms surrounding the behaviour of women are contingent both for men and for women; and, in this context, there are distinctions to be made between those who break the norms, those who tolerate the breaking of the norms, those who uphold the norms, and whether such upholders are significant or not. It is here that class and gender interact. Under changing material conditions, affecting, of course, the poorest families first, patriarchal rules about women working outside the homestead, that is, in the public sphere, break down quickly. This is especially the case for female-headed households. Thus women work as domestic servants in others' households, in the fields as agricultural labourers (perhaps increasingly invading male spheres such as harvesting, though not yet ploughing), and in rural works schemes; or they migrate to towns and cities for domestic service or industrial work, such as garment manufacture. All of these options represent varying degrees of breakdown of the cultural norms prescribing preferred behaviour for women, since mobility and increasingly unpoliced contact with non-family males will occur.

In terms of breaking the chains, however, it is important to appreciate the reactions to such behaviour for poor women. Such behaviour is the outcome of family stress, it is forced upon the family by material circumstances, and in most cases will involve decisions by men as well as by the women; indeed, in many cases, men may be encouraging reluctant women. In such situations, there is a sense in which cultural norms are being suspended rather than broken, since even the actors might prefer not to break them. The wider society can tolerate such a suspension, even though it is likely to be permanent rather than temporary, because of its enforced origins. Such suspensions are also individual, incremental decisions, whose longer-term structural implications become apparent only slowly. Ironically those segments of the society which might be the least tolerant of these survival options, which involve a breakdown or perhaps reformulation of patriarchal codes, may be precisely those classes responsible for reproducing the extreme inequalities and the deteriorating material conditions for poor families in the first place.

Such enforced breaking of the gender codes by poor women is to be contrasted with behaviour by women which is seen by men, and perhaps also by other women, as not being a necessary response to economic hardship. Obviously such a judgement about necessity is subjective. But any behaviour by women which involves their collective organization is likely to be perceived as a gratuitous challenge to male power, with women deliberately moving out of their socially constructed gender norms. Such behaviour occurs when gender relations are perceived by groups of women as chains, to be broken by establishing a new cultural basis for their status within society. This choice of perpetual deviancy from a still-preferred cultural norm about womanhood, in which respect from the keepers of patriarchal ideology has been lost, is therefore made instead of the degrading individual survival options which face poor women, as noted above.

Studies of women in the Third World, especially of poor and rural women, emphasize the problem of double exploitation through class and gender relations. Failure to acknowledge this problem is a weakness with the WID (Women in Development) position, which has tended to stress the objective of women moving into public, male-sphere forms of employment. But such a move may, of course, merely expose such women to the relationships of exploitation already experienced by poor men in these positions, in addition to their gender inferiority, which applies both at home and at work. Female workers on rural works projects may not be treated equally with men by the site managers; women in the public workforce also experience the double day, since prevailing gender relations do not release them from the primary responsibility for homestead duties. The double-day problem is likely to be even more acute for female-headed households, since such women are more likely to be seeking paid employment outside the homestead. The irony here is that those women least likely to be seeking outside work are those in extended families, where teams of women in effect reside, with the possibility of sharing homestead duties among themselves.

With these two dimensions of double exploitation and the double day, women face the difficulty of establishing a new cultural basis for the ways in which they are socially valued, with all the attendant risks for the pioneers, while remaining oppressed within the domestic culture which does not necessarily change in a corresponding manner. Thus any extension of female participation in the male, public-work sphere has to be accompanied by changes of codes not only in that sphere but in the private one too. In short, women have to fight on two fronts: within the home as well as outside it. Central to these struggles is the whole question of rights for women, *de facto* and *de jure*. The male bias in family law is an accurate reflection of the strength of patriarchal ideology in Bangladeshi society, a further superstructural shackle upon the room for female manoeuvre. A woman has to struggle, for example, over the basic procedures of divorce in this Islamic society; over her rights to property and subsistence in the event of divorce or desertion; over custody rights to children and their subsistence and education; over property rights in the event of a husband's death; over inheritance rights in her own natal family; over her rights to the dowry, which accompanies her at marriage and which affects her status in the marital home; over her rights to choose a husband, or at least veto her parents' choice; over her sexuality in marriage, determining the number of pregnancies (rape in marriage has only just been pronounced a criminal offence in the UK).

Breaking the chains for women involves challenging both what is considered appropriate female behaviour, and socially constructed gender relations. Women are obliged to establish new cultural codes through which they can gain respect and honour, while seeking to overcome the class dimensions of their poverty. Their gender is particularly hampered by survival options in the male public sphere which place them in culturally precarious situations, as well as by the patriarchal hostility to any action which attempts to assert the validity of new criteria for determining their status in the society. Gender discrimination occurs crucially within the arena of the family, where quiescent female behaviour is sustained by the woman's *de facto* weak position in the operation of family law. She has no meaningful guarantees of security outside of her dependence upon the males of both her natal and marital families. Attempts at collective solidarity with other poor females is perceived as culturally deviant even by her own menfolk, whereas the solidarity of poor males can represent an extension of masculinity, and is only considered class deviant. The situation of double exploitation for women implies double deviancy, from gender as well as class. That we have now in

Bangladesh so many examples of successful women's movements, and of women's leadership in struggles which sometimes include men, is testimony to women's unique contribution as well as to the extent of the desperation that forces them to risk so much. Other societies could learn a great deal from the strength of such women in Bangladesh.

It is no accident that a 1983 BBC Horizon programme on the social implications of agrarian change in Bangladesh and the Philippines should begin and end with the women in Proshika groups weeping over the arrest of their menfolk on charges trumped up by the landlords. Their dependency upon their men was starkly revealed. One of my most harrowing moments in Bangladesh was a visit to some poor village women in Kurigram, north Bangladesh, who had nothing to cook until their men returned from searching for work; some would be lucky on that day, others not. For many women, things have to be this bad before they can contemplate forms of action independently of their men. I recall meeting some women in Faridpur, western Bangladesh, who wanted to attend informal literacy classes in their village but had been beaten up by their husbands for wasting time. This is the reality behind the urban, middle-class feminist rhetoric of struggle. The chains are indeed wrapped around twice.

Islam in Bengal

Overlaid on class and gender relations in Bangladesh is the cultural dimension of religion, predominantly, of course, Islam. The roots of Islam in Bengali society are complex, since the respective traditions of Islam and Bengali culture have contrasting features. Without suggesting that Islam is a non-dynamic religion, it does function explicitly to uphold age- and gender-related power and authority. It is in this respect quintessentially patriarchal. The notion of brotherhood overcomes that of sisterhood, and applies strongly to the bonding of males in extended kinship structures, both real and fictive. One cannot understand loyalties, alliances, privileged transactions, interlocked markets and the informal exercise of local power relations without appreciating the role of Islam as a moral regulator and legitimizer of these relationships. An exclusively materialist discussion assumes a transparency in relationships and, therefore, a transparency of conflict and struggle which is not there. Women, particularly, suffer by this lack of transparency, but so do the poor generally. Many would argue that this subtle strength of Islam to determine and set the limits to the psychological room for manoeuvre has been intensified over recent years with the development of fundamentalist Islam across the whole of Asia. The influence of fundamentalist ideas, seeking a more obvious presence in the state through, for example, advocating the introduction of Shariat law, has been reinforced in a direct and practical way by forms of donor support from richer Islamic states.

While it would be unwise to attempt an authoritative summary of Bengali culture, there do appear to be some contrasts with the Islamic tradition and its current trends. In a nationalist and sometimes materialist sense, there has long been a radical tradition in this part of the world, campaigning against injustice not just in class terms but against cultural oppression, whether British or Urdu. East Bengal was not purely Islamic in 1947, and many who had, historically, converted to Islam had done so as an escape from the oppressions of their lowly rank and status in the Hindu caste system. The very basis of Islamic conversion was a poverty-based, radical one, an ethnic and class-based gesture. The poetry, novels and music of the religion have strongly expressed these themes of struggle for justice and national identity, and continue to do so. The passionate expression of such themes has been, and is, paralleled by action. Bengal is famous for its political movements, its opposition to colonial rule in all forms (dependence upon foreign aid is a cause of deep embarrassment for many in Bangladesh), its demonstrations on the streets, its clandestine revolutionaries, but also for its essential humanism acted out in the creative establishment of welfare societies and development institutions. None of this is recent; witness the combination of ideas and practical action in Tagore. In West Bengal such themes have reached centre stage in the policy making and implementation in the Left Front state government. With contemporary global developments in Islam, such ambitions are more difficult to achieve in Bangladesh where Islam continues to reveal itself as a conservative rather than as a radical social force. But the sheer creativity of the Bengali spirit, often rooted in the deep suffering of a precarious agrarian system where necessity is the mother of invention, will ensure that the struggle to break chains continues.

Agrarian conditions for struggle

The conditions of this struggle have to be contextualized further in terms of a broader understanding of the agrarian structure and the directions which it might be taking. Although the application of class to an analysis of such struggle has been discussed and refined earlier, along with gender, and although distinctions have been made between protest and revolution, we still have to consider the structural circumstances in which the mobilization of the poor takes place. Two major principles must be established: first, Bangladesh is not homogeneous with respect to its agrarian structure; second, these differing structures are changing quite rapidly, with implications for class and gender configurations.

Regional diversity

The first of these principles can be dealt with quite briefly and can be considered further in Wood (1981), 'Rural Class Formation in Bangladesh 1940–80'. The earlier agrarian studies during the 1960s were based to a large extent upon the experience of Comilla, and conducted through the Academy for Rural Development. However, the Dhaka-Comilla belt, that is the region east of Dhaka up to the Indian border, was historically the most fertile area of the country and the most densely settled. As mentioned earlier, this resulted in a distinctive small-farmer rural economy with a low average level of landholding, few significant landlords and sharecroppers, and a low incidence of landlessness. The Comilla co-operative experiment arose out of this socio-economic configuration. In short, the proposition was being advanced that no significant class differentiation existed and consequently there was no need for class-based forms of struggle. It was further assumed that the whole of deltaic Bangladesh could be regarded in these terms.

Two problems emerge at this point. In the regions of the country outside this socio-ecological belt, the picture was different, and even within the smallholder region relationships of exploitation existed, especially through usurious moneylending. Elsewhere, especially to the north and west, greater inequalities in landholding were evident, with classic landlord–tenant relations and an increasing scale of landlessness. The form of exploitation here was control over land, expressed through rents and depressed wages. The separation of the population by class was also more coterminous with its separation by kin and residential locality. Here the *bangsho* acted more clearly as the proxy of caste, with the lines of conflict of interest and potential struggle consequently more sharply drawn. The NGOs emerging in the 1970s drew their experience from these sorts of situations, within a tradition of radical political parties and peasant associations. Such parties had nevertheless restricted themselves to a rhetorical leadership style, seeking instant mass support for land reform and wage increases. The NGOs, on the other hand, realised that even in areas divided sharply by class and kin, the poor could not be expected just to join mass movements and threaten their immediate livelihoods. At the same time, they certainly rejected what they regarded as the hopeless revisionism of the Comilla approach as totally inappropriate to the economic and political needs of the poor.

Agrarian future: fragmentation, landlessness and entrepreneurial opportunities

The second principle, concerning the structure and patterns of contemporary agrarian change, is much more important as the context in which the struggles outlined in this book took place, and as a guide to an agenda of struggle and opportunities in the future.

In Bangladesh, the annual rate of population growth is considered to be about 2.5 per cent. The overall area is 144 000 sq km, of which 63 per cent is cultivable. The population density of the cultivated area is now in excess of 1150 per sq km. For a population which is 90 per cent rural and mainly dependent upon agriculture, this is high. The significance of this figure must, of course, be modified by recognizing that about 40 per cent of the cultivated area is double-cropped and 8 per cent triple-cropped. While projected urbanization for Bangladesh is alarming, this population density, together with rising landlessness, has not resulted so far in a dramatic increase in urbanization. Discounting changing definitions, the rate of urban growth since 1974 has been about 6 per cent per year. There has been a marked gender imbalance to this process, with a sex ratio of 151 males per 100 women in Chittagong, 139 in Dhaka and 133 in Khulna, with an overall sex ratio in the country of 106. This gender imbalance reveals a process of rural males in search of urban work – seasonal imbalances are, of course, much higher – leaving women, as mothers, sisters, wives or daughters, to survive from rural production or labour. Perhaps the most general consequence of population pressure is not urban expression but rural settlement on marginal lands liable to flooding, especially in the disaster-prone coastal areas.

With a predominantly rural population, highly dependent upon agriculture, poverty is a function of access: first to cultivable land and second to employment opportunities in the countryside. As noted above, patron classes dominate both. With the narrow industrial and manufacturing base, the prospects for urban employment are restricted. The ramifications of the population growth remain, therefore, concentrated within the agrarian structure. Larger families are living off the same or reduced size holding, so that there are about 3 million farms with holdings above 2.5 acres and in excess of 3 million farms with a smaller acreage. The high fragmentation of holdings reflects the kin-ecology outcomes of multiple inheritance, in effect between sons, so that over 60 per cent of farms consists of more than 6 plots, with 10 per cent of farms having more than 20 plots.

With this increase in fragmentation and the decline in family farm size, below-subsistence peasants are steadily dispossessed through mortgage, debt and distress sale. The viability of such smallholdings depends increasingly upon the availability of land to sharecrop, but, with double cropping, such opportunities have become largely seasonal rather than annual, and involve higher-risk investments in modern methods to which the poor have only precarious and expensive access. The increase in landlessness, which has resulted from this process of dispossesion and insecure tenancy, has been variously estimated, with some consensus that around 70 per cent of rural households do not possess enough land for subsistence and rely upon wage labour in agriculture, rural works or outmigration.

This rise in landlessness, together with the decrease in the average size of holding down to precarious levels for the majority of remaining landholders, has increased the value to the family of male children as income earners and providers of old-age security, since work opportunities, though limited, are in the public sphere. This has depressed the real value of rural wages, except in the peak seasons of new production. Since only the poorest women are culturally permitted to enter the public sphere for manual work, daughters-in-law from other families have, under these conditions, been transformed from labour assets in the hitherto self-sufficient farm to consumption burdens in the majority of remaining precarious households. This contributes to the explanation of recent, steady increases in the practice and value of dowry, as compensation for the receiving family. The steady increase in those seeking work in rural labour markets, including the poorest women, has created a reserve army of underemployed labour, undermining the patron's need for clients. Wage exploitation is intensified, though labour is freed at the same time. Under these conditions however, the freeing of labour does not lead to the creation of a proletariat to break the chains, but rather to that of a fragmented underclass.

The consequences of this pressure upon the land in the context of restricted alternative employment opportunities should be understood in terms of other developments in the agrarian structure, which might be summed up as 'agrarian entrepreneurialism' (Wood 1991). For a variety of reasons, some attributed to the sub-colonial status of East Bengal within Pakistan, in the period up to the end of the 1970s rural class relations in Bangladesh were dominated by the use of capital in the sphere of exchange, such as renting, moneylending and trading, rather than through the expansion of production. This certainly raised the level of absolute surplus value accruing to certain classes, but did not contribute to the development of productive capital among landowners. The failure during this period to develop productive agricultural capital has resulted in the increases in landlessness and rural underemployment, and in the depression of real wage rates. This has created a problem of effective demand among the increasing proportion of rural people obliged to purchase foodgrains, thereby undermining price incentives required to stimulate owners of land into raising productivity. Up to the end of the 1970s, this situation was in effect reinforced by a strategy of state-administered subsidies to agriculture, which were intended to stimulate production. The strategy was implemented through the Bangladesh Agricultural Development Corporation (BADC), which controlled both imports of chemical inputs and equipment, especially mechanized irrigation units, and their distribution through outlets at district and sub-district levels. With subsidies, state monopoly and restricted access, corruption, alongside high default rates and under-utilization of equipment, was widespread.

The state, with its monopoly control over external capital, had become in effect an arena within which funds were diverted into modes of parasitic surplus extraction through an alliance of central and local bureaucratic officials with their favoured clients in the countryside.

It was clear that any expansion in agricultural investment would be dependent upon external aid, and both the World Bank and USAID, as the major donors at that time, were determined, through their diagnoses and leverage, to liberate the rural economy from bureaucratic management and control by encouraging open market systems of food and input distribution. Their strategy, which became the strategy for Bangladesh during the 1980s, consisted of: open-market dealing in food (through procurement at market rates, storage in a network of *godowns*, and release of stocks into local markets triggered by a 20 per cent variance in seasonal prices); the phasing out of fertilizer and other input subsidies (for example on various forms of mechanized irrigation); coupled with a major emphasis on HYV technologies in rice and wheat. These efforts concentrated on the improvement of foodgrain supply, with a noticeable lack of attention to the structure of demand for food. The strategy involved the assumption that a combination of support prices for foodgrains, through a generous procurement price, and open-market dealing in rural goods (inputs and food) would encourage the landholders to raise the productivity of their land, thereby increasing their marketable surplus to pay the full market price for inputs.

Looking at the performance of these policies during ithe 1980s, the annual rate of growth in agriculture was about 3 per cent during the first half (contrasted to the 6.5 per cent planned), and dipped in the second half to nearer 2 per cent. A UNDP 'nationalist' study in the late 1980s was keen to attribute this to policy, though the floods of 1987 and 1988 will have had some impact. The more input-dependent crops, such as wheat and HYV *boro* (winter rice), which have been responsible for the expansion since 1980s, have shown signs of losing momentum due to irrigation failure, farmer preferences for rotations, decline in fertilizer/yield coefficients, and early flooding on late harvested crops. The slow rate of growth in foodgrain production is partially explained by slower rates of expansion in the irrigated area than targeted. But even these rates of growth in foodgrain production have been difficult to achieve.

Although fertilizer use has risen by over 30 per cent, its price to the farmer has risen by over 150 per cent while the prices of the two major crops, rice and jute, have only risen by about 50 per cent. Such adverse terms of trade to the farmer may well have depressed the potential use of fertilizer over the period. Furthermore, per capita foodgrains availability has still not reached pre-independence levels (160kg compared to 177). In other words, Bangladesh is still further away from food self-sufficiency than it was 20 years ago.

It must be noted further that a significant proportion of the increase in foodgrain production has been achieved through the expansion of acreage devoted to foodgrains rather than a dramatic increase in yields, which seem to have reached a plateau. Thus about 1.0 million acres of jute has been diverted to rainfed cereals; and about 1.5 million acres of winter pulses and oilseeds diverted to wheat and winter rice. This reveals a society under considerable stress, with anxieties about crop diversification and the implications of this cereal displacement upon diet and the import bill.

These agricultural trends during the 1980s (and many commentators have made similar summaries and observations) have structural implications for the agrarian system which establishes the conditions under which the poor in Bangladesh must find options for survival. Despite the many institutional and technical constraints to agricultural growth, we must acknowledge the current path of a significant and continuing expansion of capital in agriculture. This consists of further expansion of mechanized irrigation to intensify land use, a marked recent trend in the use of power tillers (with added extensions for such activities as road and boat transportation, or rice milling), a continuation in the use of chemical inputs, the use of conventional tractors, and so on. In this process, there is a proliferation of actors in the agricultural system, which has the potential of reducing the significance of the family farm, whether large or small, tenanted or owned, in the distribution of agrarian power. Boyce (1987:37) defines agrarian structure as 'the subset of institutions governing the distribution of rights in agricultural means of production, notably land. These rights include not only ownership, but also such arrangements as tenancy and mortgage, which create a divergence between ownership and actual operation'. With this definition and the preceding observations in mind, we are witnessing the addition of non-cultivators and non-landowners to this subset of institutions.

As noted earlier, this proliferation is occurring under general economic conditions which constrain families from leaving agriculture for other sectors of the economy. It is also the case that the rise of landlessness cannot be equated with a simple process of polarization in landholding. Population growth and the multiple inheritance principle in the division of holdings (maintained by the absence of alternative employment prospects) act as a constraint to the development of large farms, and certainly consolidated ones. This combination of conditions entails the extreme fragmentation of family cultivable land into different plots. These are scattered over the village reflecting divisions at the time of inheritance on the basis of not only area, but also of soil type and elevation.

With the continuing importance of irrigation to family survival, through enabling the intensification of land use, it remains imperative that the division of holdings is equal in all respects. The capitalization of agriculture thus acts as a stimulant to farm fragmentation, although some of the technologies associated with that process are usually regarded as demanding consolidation to reduce lumpiness. Thus, since this fragmentation is structurally inherent to the conditions in Bangladesh, the contradiction between fragmentation and the technological requirements of agricultural growth can only be resolved by separating the ownership of land from the actual operation of it with the new technologies.

In this process, non-land packages of capital, led especially by the control over water, become the more consolidated assets. Fragmentation may have been a problem for conventional thinking on farm and land management, prompting attempts at consolidation of holdings, but seen in this way it actually constitutes an institutional opportunity to those who control these non-land packages of capital and who make up the proliferation of actors noted above. While it is true that richer families can more easily diversify into these non-cultivating, but agricultural roles of delivering such services as irrigation, ploughing, processing and transportation, the principle is established that surplus value from agriculture can be obtained without owning land, through the provision of services.

Although the central importance of irrigation has been emphasized, because of its significance to the intensification of land use under demographic pressures, control over water is not alone in this process. There are increasing examples of fertilizer delivery and pesticide spraying, undertaken as a commercial service by command area 'managers', often using contract labour. With the increase in mechanized milling and the likely widespread introduction of power tillers, fragmented plots will be consolidated not around individual household units (the 'Punjab' model), but around the owners (single or collective) of production, processing and transportation technologies (the 'Bangladesh' model). The concept of 'command area' is not then restricted to irrigation sources. Whether coterminous or not, areas of land will be in the command of other packages of mechanical and chemical technologies, and vertically organized marketing arrangements. Even without considering a large-scale processing sector (for example large rice and sugar mills, potato cold storage or tobacco management), the existing levels of production and food processing capital can combine in the formation of agricultural companies loosely networked or corporate, interlinked with repair workshops, mechanics services, supplies of spare parts and fuel, transportation and marketing. In this Bangladesh model, the family farm declines as a socio-economic entity while the agricultural system becomes re-articulated through these other units of production and exchange.

At this stage, this analysis should not be pushed too far. Three factors offset this logical outcome in which the Bangladesh farm disappears altogether in favour of agricultural companies which develop a complete control of land use:

o Larger farms are able to allocate larger absolute amounts of land to crops other than irrigation dependent ones, and have less need to intensify land use by demanding services from others.

o New strategies for tenancy and mortgaging have emerged, in which poorer farmers may counteract their lack of capital, or 'lumpy' technology problems in technologically dependent seasons by leasing out land to those sufficiently well networked or capitalized to use it (reverse, seasonal tenancy: Glaser 1989). Mortgaging can also achieve a similar result. Poorer farmers can also lease in seasonally to offset their marginalization.

o Apparently lumpy technologies can be socially broken down and mediated into the needs of small, individual customers. Lewis (1991) has noted this process for tractors in Comilla.

Land: the fading asset

The importance of this grounded speculation about the evolving agrarian structure in Bangladesh to breaking the chains centres on the implications of this scenario for empowerment and employment options facing the poor. The issue here is the purpose of action. There can be no doubt that the key problem is the provision for mass employment at wage rates which deliver at least subsistence incomes. It is obvious that there can be no single solution to this. Urban employment in the industrial and services sectors can only make a limited contribution for the foreseeable future; likewise the rural 'non-farm' sector, which has meant in Bangladesh rural works programmes to support the landless during seasonal troughs in the demand for agricultural labour. However, the potentiality of the non-farm agricultural sector has been largely overlooked, yet it contains opportunities not just for expanded employment in more open-market conditions but also for a realignment of power.

When the concentration of the historically central means of production, land, which has determined power and authority for centuries in the Bengal countryside, is becoming diffused in the manner noted above, then the circumstances in which struggle takes place are also changing profoundly. It becomes important to understand which battles have become anachronistic, and which retain their relevance to the present and foreseeable future. In the scenario outlined above, does it make sense to encourage the poor into struggles for land reform? The rhetoric about landlords and the need for a redistributive land reform is hopelessly out of date, and we do the poor no favours by clinging to redundant slogans. For example, the process of agrarian change outlined here offers the prospect of steering these agrarian entrepreneurial activities towards the landless, where they can gain rents and profits from expanded agricultural production; that is, not just employment but empowerment to enhance their rights and status in ever-widening arenas. The purpose of action for the landless can thus look beyond the prospects of more field-level employment under intensified land-use conditions for a declining proportion of new entrants to the labour force (where increasing proportions of family labour will be used anyway). At the same time, the landless need not be beguiled into false expectations of becoming landowners themselves. This is not to deny the value of certain kinds of land-acquisition struggles, for example over *khas* land (untitled land in the formal disposition of government) or ponds – but such programmes have to be placed in perspective. They represent in most cases a one-off opportunity in any locality (since the status of such land most often arose out of migrations, from 1947 onwards until 1972), and such land constitutes a tiny proportion of cultivable land resources in the country. While rewarding for those involved among groups and their NGOs, such land reform does not impinge upon the main structural problems for the future.

Proshika, groups and the case studies

As a prelude to the case studies in this volume, which consist of experiences from groups organized with the support of Proshika, some further description of Proshika's approach to development and the poor is appropriate. Towards the end of this discussion, it will also be appropriate to note that while Proshika has organised its empowerment and employment strategies around the scenario for Bangladesh's agrarian future, as outlined in the preceding sections, it has alternative scenarios for the future which it seeks to promote. Such alternatives consist critically of organic substitutes for chemically dependent paths to agricultural development. If successful, and widespread, then the implications for the configuration of power within the society are also profound.

The name Proshika is a contraction of three concepts: *proshikshan* (training), *shiksa* (development education), and *kaj* (action). Proshika *Manobik Unnayan Kendra* is then translated as Proshika, a Centre for Human Development. It was established to help increase the level of socio-economic efficiency of landless workers, women and men, marginal peasants and other poor people in Bangladesh (now urban as well as rural, though the examples in these case studies are rural) by forming groups to build up their unity and organization; providing knowledge and skills through human development and skills training; and assisting the groups through loans and technical support to develop employment and income-generating activities. By early 1992, Proshika had mobilized in excess of 25 000 groups through nearly 50 Area Development Centres (ADCs), distributed across 75 out of 400 *upazila*. About 50 per cent of the groups consists exclusively of women. It currently employs nearly 900 staff (*kurmi*), distributed between the ADCs, the Training Centre at Koitta (30 miles west of Dhaka), and the HQ in Dhaka.

Proshika sees a strong link between the local unity of the poor and activities that, in providing a degree of material independence, assist the poor in counteracting the structures responsible for their poverty that is, wage rates, tenant shares, interest rates, concentrated access to land and water (drinking, irrigation and fishery), other means of production, means of transportation, production skills, education and health. In this sense, Proshika's activities have to be seen as mutually reinforcing. These activities consist of group formation, conscientization, through informal processes of development education, training (activity skills, management practices, literacy and health), social action (on wages, tenant shares, occupation of *khas* land, leasing *bheels* and ponds for fishing, and provision of pure drinking water through hand tube wells, and income generation, such as livestock raising, vegetable growing, roadside and social forestry, sericulture, apiculture, fishing, provision of irrigation services, milling, often supported by credit from a Revolving Loan Fund (RLF). In pursuit of these aims, Proshika is committed to experimental action research programmes which involve institutional innovation. As far as possible, its methods are participatory, with initiatives arising from open discussions between group members and the field staff. Ideas and programmes are never imposed upon the groups, though sometimes the enthusiasms of the members may not be supported by Proshika.

An example of this style is the organic agricultural alternatives scenario, noted earlier. This programme is currently in its infancy but respresents a fundamental challenge to HYV high-tech approaches to agriculture which are disarticulating the rural economy, as described in the fragmentation and entrepreneurialism discussion. This programme of promoting smallholder, integrated sustainability is designed to be both environmentally friendly and to provide a degree of economic independence as a platform for other struggles. It consists of integrating homestead horticulture with livestock rearing, small-scale fisheries and organic arable farming where such crop land is still available. If successful, it will have the effect of reducing the dependent interaction of such marginal and small peasants with the market for chemical and some mechanical inputs. At the same time, it hopes to demonstrate that higher, sustainable yields can be achieved through recycling own waste and crop residues. This will enable poor farmers and homestead holders to obtain and retain agricultural surplus for sale at non-harvest prices and thereby purchase consumer goods without encountering the usual adverse terms of trade incurred when they are obliged to sell at low immediate post-harvest prices to repay credit.

The further impact of such a programme would be to delay the process of landlessness which arises from fragmentation of holdings into non-viable units, and to increase the degree of autonomous management over land use. The traditional peasant role of conservers and trustees of the land for future generations will be rediscovered. The programme may also encourage new settlement patterns where, under appropriate topographical circumstances, small peasants may be prepared to move their homesteads to be adjacent to remaining arable land. If this were to happen, there would be a profound effect upon political and authority dynamics in the village as people moved from marginal sites and away from the control of *para* leaders.

There is, of course, a long way to go with such a programme, but elements of it are already being pursued by different households within the groups. It is supported by considerable on-site experimentation at the Proshika Training Centre at Koitta, which has now expanded its area to include arable land. The possibilities of integrating fish and paddy are also known, and the impact of extended livestock and horticulture upon diet is welcomed. With urbanization and the proliferation of non-primate cities, the market for such produce is most likely to be significantly extended for those in these scattered urban hinterlands. The various arguments in favour of this approach to agrarian reform all contribute to the central objective of empowerment, especially the disengagement from certain input markets.

However, this summary of Proshika's approach loses some of its distinctive flavour. The NGO's founders were intimately caught up in the personal and domestic traumas of the liberation struggle, some fleeing into refugee camps, others remaining by choice or default in precarious positions within the country during the Pakistan crack-down, and others joining the liberation struggle directly. Although this is an experience which is now 20 years old, its significance should not be diminished by commentators. Such intense dislocation and insecurity at the beginning of one's adult life will strongly influence the rest of it. This was the case to a lesser degree for myself, across the border in Bihar during the liberation war, when I witnessed the final battle quite closely and visited the refugee camps on the border before the final denouement. I also witnessed with them the first years of liberated Bangladesh, which were almost as insecure and anarchical, with an arbitrary government clearly out of control amidst a biblical famine of horrific dimensions. The sense of betrayal and shame was acute.

We have to remember that much of this experience was also shared by the people in the villages, though young urban intellectuals were singled out particularly for harsh treatment. This means that when Proshika started, there was no pre-set single idea, like welfare delivery or credit. Instead, the early contacts among the poor and the organization's founders matured together. Proshika's approach evolved through these shared experiences and sense of affinity. All were amateurs, feeling their way into analysis and solution, sure then only of one fact: the poor peasantry had been mobilized for liberation but not for a revolution, the government was abdicating its responsibilities to the poor from the outset.

Over time, of course, a strategy has developed. Proshika has expanded; new staff have been recruited from a younger generation; new groups are constantly being formed; the proportion of women's groups is rising; amateurs have become professionals in mobilization, training, technical interventions, research and management; more donors have joined in enlarged budgets; government has listened on different issues, most recently on social forestry; other, smaller NGOs have been supported; networks within the region have been developed; research and consultancy services have been provided; credit supported income-generating projects have been expanded. But the achievement of which Proshika is most proud is none of these, despite their obvious importance and value. Rather the sense of achievement lies most strongly in the kinds of struggles recorded in this volume and the development of people's organizations, which are federations of groups with their own leaders.

This statement will annoy many in the development business. Where are the hard indicators of poverty impact and alleviation? What are the rates of return on credit disbursed? How many people are reached with what resources? What is the staff-group ratio, and is it declining? Have Proshika staff successfully withdrawn from original areas? Are groups sustainable? What is the sex-ratio of benefits? Are we sure that efforts are devoted only to the poorest (quintile, decile)? While Proshika is equipped to deal with these questions, refuting their validity in some cases, they are not of fundamental concern and they fail to engage with the organization's roots and its analysis of poverty. All the current development management jargon, with all the institutions and interests entailed by it, is essentially based upon the efficacy of service delivery. At best, the jargon should be 'welfare' management. This discourse is fashionable just now, as it was for African administrative reform in the 1970s, that is before structural adjustment was invented in the 1980s.

But the discourse is pernicious, even when it includes participatory rhetoric, because it suggests solutions independent of the structures which produce the problems. These structures are the chains described in this volume. Empowerment among the poor is the only route to the destruction of these chains and thus the preparation for fair shares in the allocation of global and national public revenues. These propositions cannot be dismissed as the clichés of unreconstructed Marxists just because the language is embarrassing in the contemporary lap-top world of the enterprise culture. Neither Proshika nor the poor with whom it works are fooled by this. Hence the weight given to the evidence of struggle reported in this volume and the development of people's organizations, which has occurred since these studies were collected. Certainly I prefer this evidence to the consensus emerging in Bangladesh (and expressed forcefully in a recent Planning Commission seminar in January 1992), from the analysis of poverty-focused employment and income-generating projects, that 75 per cent of such expenditure (mainly aid-sourced) is consumed by the upper 50 per cent in the society in order to deliver 25 per cent to the lower 50 per cent. And we can be sure that the distribution within these broad bands is highly skewed. The qualitative evidence of poverty structures being changed is significant in developmental terms rather than in a short-term welfare sense. It is a sad fact of life that those responsible for changing oppressive structures are finally those who are oppressed. This is the principle of Proshika's work, and it remains in first place on its agenda for the society as a whole.

References

E. Banfield (1958) *The Moral Basis Of a Backward Society*

J. Boyce (1987) *Agrarian Impasse in Bengal: Institutional Constraints to Technological Change* Oxford University Press

M. Glaser (1989) *Water to the Swamp: Patterns of Accumulation from Irrigation to Rajshahi Villages* Ph.D thesis, University of Bath, UK

A. Huq (ed.) (1976, 1978) *Exploitation and the Rural Poor*, BARD, Comilla (7 out 9 chs by G. Wood)

D. Lewis (1991) *Technology and Transactions* Centre for Social Studies, Dhaka University

S. White (1992) *Arguing with the Crocodile: Gender and Class in Rural Bangladesh*, Zed Books.

G. Wood (1981) 'Rural Class Formation in Bangladesh 1940–1980', *Bulletin of Concerned Asian Scholars* 13, 4

—— (1991) 'Agrarian Entrepreneurialism in Bangladesh', *Indian Journal of Labour Economics* 34, 1: 13–27

GEOFFREY D. WOOD
Dhaka, January 1992 (revised April 1992)

PART II: CASE STUDIES

The typical citizen of Bangladesh is the landless or poor peasant of the village, far from the video-flooded capital. The rural population is 87 per cent in a country heavily dominated by agriculture and the number of landless, estimated at 60 per cent of the rural population, is increasing rapidly. The vast majority of the villagers have no access to the surrounding resources and the inequalities between rich and poor are widening.

This polarization is a result of the prevailing power structure of rural Bangladesh and is a man-made development, not caused by floods or cyclones. The rich are getting richer and the poor poorer and increasing in number. Ultimately, it is a question whether the poor are to succeed in mobilizing for their survival.

> The nature of the relationship in which people are involved as regards credit, mortgage, sharecropping, employment and political protection is to a large extent of a vertical patron-client nature. During the next few decades, the social organization of the rural areas could well continue to be dominated by this structure. Even though there are relationships of a horizontal nature among patrons, there is hardly any such relationship among clients. Rich peasants support each other and make alliances with government officials and the urban elite. Poor people seldom unite for specific purposes or support each other. The future direction of the social organization in rural Bangladesh will depend, to a large extent, on the development of socio-political consciousness among the rural poor. (*Rural poverty in Bangladesh. A report to the like-minded group, a summary*, p. 24. Universities Research Centre 1 January 1986)

Proshika is one of several NGOs working among the rural poor. PROSHIKA stands for *proshikshan* — Training, *shiksa* — Development education and *kaj* — Action. Within Proshika there are some 25,000 organized groups, which implies nearly half a million members. About fifty per cent of them are women. Half a million may sound like a very small number in a country of 120 million, but it is a critical mass to influence society at local and national levels.

Very briefly, the ideology and strategy of Proshika is as follows. Poverty does not only mean that a person is without resources, it also implies that the poverty-striken loses self-confidence and belief in her or his own capabilities or potential. She or he turns into a fatalist, devoid of power. Human development, in the concept of Proshika, aims to make the impoverished understand that it is they themselves who are the force capable of changing their situation. They have to take charge over their own development, unite and organize on their own class basis. Collective efforts are emphasized as well as the building of solidarity and mutual help. They have to develop a critical consciousness so they can understand, analyse and recognize their role in society and their relationship to the rural power structure. Proshika also implies a gradual diminution of their dependence on the existing power structure, through developing their own unity in their own organizations and economic ventures. One way of achieving this is by organization and mobilization for social justice, fair wages or government-owned resources; another is regular collective savings and economic projects.

The following case studies hopefully give a better picture. While moving from one village to another, sitting down discussing with those who have organized, one cannot but be impressed and hopeful. The impoverished have started organizing and fighting back. They have just started their struggle for living in human circumstances and for dignity. They know what it is all about. It is a conscious fight for the lives and futures of their children.

Greater solidarity for greater power

In Shibgonj *upazila* in Bogra District 80 per cent of the population, as in most parts of Bangladesh, are dependent on agriculture. Sixty per cent of the rural population are landless labourers or marginal farmers.

In 1979 Proshika started organizing the landless and marginal farmers in groups consisting of an average of 20 members. According to Proshika development ideology and practice it is of great importance that people organize from the smaller, group level and then expand, from group level to village, further to union level and thereafter to *upazila* level, co-ordinating actions and mobilization.

The strength of the organized lies in their unity and large numbers. Co-ordination is essential if they are to succeed in obtaining their social rights. Establishment of the legal right to *khas* resources, obtaining legal wages, the abolition of the dowry system and actions against corrupt government officials can never be achieved by a single group; broader mobilization is essential.

The organized group members know from experience that without this group solidarity they cannot successfully pursue their demands or consolidate their group strength. This experience is based on several concrete issues. In the area there are more than a thousand *khas* ponds, which are illegally occupied by the local élites in the name of village property. According to the law these ponds are to be leased out to the landless. When groups came to know about this right through human development training, they decided to act to get control over some of these ponds, with two results: firstly, this was the first time the power structure of the élite had been challenged by the lower strata of local society; secondly it meant that economic resources were transferred from the local rich to the organized landless. The immediate reaction of the vested interests was traditional. By using force and influence, by filing false cases and conspiracies, by harassment in co-operation with the police, the élite tried to re-establish their total power over both the resources and the people. The only way for the organized to counter this was to increase their numbers and their strength.

In 1983 the Proshika ADC in Shibgonj had 300 organized groups. Although there were still many villages to cover, village and union level co-ordination committees to be formed and considerable basic work to be done, the pressing social problems pushed the organized groups to start planning a larger organization. In an advanced group leadership training course they decided to create a forum representing all of the organized groups.

At the initial stage 60 group leaders met and formulated a plan to assemble representatives from all groups. Three hundred group leaders attended a meeting to form a committee consisting of the 60 village co-ordination leaders which was entrusted with the responsibility of formulating an overall programme for the larger group. The programme was presented after four meetings.

The co-ordinating group was called Mojur Mukti, meaning Labourers' Freedom, and its task was to organize groups in areas which Proshika workers did not have time to visit. It was also responsible for forming functioning village and union level co-ordination organizations and setting up an annual conference. They made a charter of demands: to get *khas* land according to government law; to get other legal facilities such as education, health care and minimum wages. They started publicizing dowry and divorce issues and promoting marriage without dowry within the organized groups.

Every year since its formation, the Mojur Mukti arranges an annual conference on 8 March. In 1986 it took place on a playground in front of a school two miles from the Shibgonj *upazila* headquarters.

It was late spring and so hot that it was impossible to remain in the sun. There were a couple of chairs and a table, with a large piece of cloth stretched over it, in one corner of the field which, at the most, would provide shade for a thousand people. The rest had to find shelter from the sun, themselves sitting in the shadows of the surrounding trees.

The food was prepared in another corner of the field — large quantities of a mix of rice, pulses, potatoes, onion and spices, called *khechuri*. Cooking started the night before to be sure of providing enough food for all the expected participants.

In front of the table was a microphone, and two loudspeakers were hung on the poles in the shade. Banners in red and white were hanging here and there with slogans like, 'All landless unite!', 'Long live Mojur Mukti!' and 'We want just wages!'

Processions of men and women began to arrive at 11am, carrying banners and battery-powered loudspeakers through which they shouted their slogans. Many had been marching and chanting for several hours, making their voices husky or broken. By 12.30 the entire field was full of enthusiastic people, who had come from all corners of the *upazila*. In all there were 5000 participants, some 700 of them women. Almost all of them were group members, but some unorganized landless and marginal farmers also participated.

One group member was elected chairman to preside over the conference. The conference started with a Muslim member reciting the Holy Koran and a Hindu member reciting from the *Bhagavadgita*. This is not very common. The general practice is to recite the Holy Koran only but the conference tried to uphold secularism.

Then the speeches began. One talked about the *khas* issue; how the groups of his area were confronting the rich who illegally occupied the *khas* land. He blamed the government officials who collaborate with the local élites. Another talked about the lack of health facilities; how the doctors ignore the poor people, how 'free' medicine has to be bought from the market because the government health complexes have insufficient allotted medicine. A third took up the education issue; he blamed the teachers of being more interested in earning money as private tutors for the children of the rich than giving education to the poor children of the village. Another spoke about the police; how the police act in the interest of the rich, how the bribes are making the police act against the law in cases of access to *khas* resources.

A woman spoke about dowry; how men sometimes behaved with women, how much work women do without any recognition and how women are tortured and killed because the dowry is not paid. The dowry idea was taken from rich people and she demanded that the practice stop among the rural poor. She described how groups in her locality were fighting against dowry and successfully arranging marriages among group members and their families. She called all participants of the conference to stand up and follow their example.

Another woman talked about divorce, explaining the sufferings of the women when they are divorced. One of the reasons for divorce is poverty because a new marriage may mean money and sometimes wealth for the man. She called on everybody, especially the men, to direct their fight against poverty and exploitation, not against women.

A man also raised the issue of women's situation in society. Men are often ignorant of how much the women contribute to the family. Equality between women and men was important in their struggle. An organized, conscious man should not beat his wife.

The next speaker made the crowd laugh although he talked seriously, about the perpetual exploitation of the landless, the élite's misbehaviour and misdoings, but managed to describe the cruelties towards the poor with humour. He impersonated a landlord when talking about one. His way of acting out some of the funny sides of the rich and powerful made their image less superior and beyond understanding, showing that humour is an important weapon.

Another talked in terms of the poor developing their own, nonformal education system instead of being dependent on the nonfunctioning government system. According to his experience groups were able to do their own literacy training and he offered the programme developed in his area to any other interested groups.

While the meeting was going on two policemen appeared and tried to find who the organizer of this large gathering was by asking the people in the outskirts of the crowd, but the surrounding people hushed them and listened intently to the speeches. After some time the police left.

The speeches were an inventory of the vast experience of the many organized groups and demonstrated an annual possibility of developing co-operation and solidarity within the movement and of sharing experiences and ideas. One Proshika worker also made a speech. He emphasized the working people's unity and the importance of leading their own development efforts and struggle for their rights.

It was late afternoon when the 1986 Shibgonj Mojur Mukti Conference came to an end. A few songs were presented, written by group members, which called for joint organization and the fight for a better future.

When dusk fell the conference chairman told the delegates to get ready for the food. Banana leaves, to be used as plates, were distributed and the queue to the only hand-tubewell available grew rapidly. In peaceful order all the 5000 sat down in lines. While the *khechuri* was served, the sun set.

This greater organization building is being developed in all areas where Proshika is working. In some areas it is already quite advanced, while in others it is still in its infancy. These case studies tell the story of some of the groups' efforts.

Fights for legal control of *khas* resources

Khas *ponds*

Purbo Para Bhumihin Samity (the Eastern Para Landless Society) and Mudhu Para Bhumihin Samity (the Middle Para Landless Society) were formed in 1981. The two groups consist of 28 and 29 members respectively. They are located in Tial village, Shibgonj *upazilla*, Bogra District. In the village there are two more organized landless *samitys*, women's groups with a total of 28 members. The four groups have regular weekly meetings and their subscriptions are one taka per person per week.

The men's groups have carried through a number of economical projects. Like nearly every Proshika group, they started by investing their savings in income-generating activities, on a small scale at first but increasing as profits from successful ventures were reinvested in new schemes. The two groups bought a second-hand low lift pump in 1985 paying 14 000 taka from their savings funds and earlier profits. Some of the members received training in pump operation and maintenance from Proshika. By selling irrigation facilities to farmers for the rabi crop (the winter season high-yielding variety of paddy) they had a net income of 5000 taka during the first year.

Since the groups were formed in 1981 they have been heavily involved in cattle rearing. Over the years they have invested a total of 15 000 taka in cattle. Today the two groups collectively own some 40 cows, bullocks and calves which give them a substantial extra income on top of their meagre earnings as day labourers.

In 1982 they started recovery of the four *khas* ponds in the area, all of which cover less than an acre each. The story of this action is typical of such claims. The usual local practice was that those who had the means (nets and other resources) caught the fish, but always in the name of the whole village community. Poor people did not have the means to take part in the catch so it was controlled by the rich, for their profit.

After the *samitys* were formed the members found out from Proshika training that *khas* ponds were supposed to be distributed to the local landless. They soon organized to gain control over the *khas* resources of their area. They started by occupying the pond situated closest to their houses and invested 500 taka in fish fry. Later, during monsoon, the pond was flooded and they lost a lost of the fish, but they had enough to sell to raise 4500 taka. More importantly they had been able to improve their family diets by eating fish from the pond. In the last two years they have earned 14 000 taka from selling fish, although the pond has been flooded every year.

They also tried to get control over the other three ponds but have only succeeded in taking two of them. They were prevented from taking the last one by the local landlords and the chairman. In 1982 the landlords came to the site intending to attack the group members while they were fishing, but decided not to act because there were not enough of them.

In the following year, the two groups sought co-operation with a third organized group in a neighbouring village to get control over the third pond, so that when they went to fish there were nearly 100 organized landless. This time they were attacked by more than 1000 people, headed by the chairman. Four members were seriously injured in the clash while two from the other side suffered injuries. Women's groups in the area also took part in the clash, defending the interests of the landless.

After the clash the conflict continued, with the landlords filing a case against 16 of the group members and two of the Proshika *kurmis*, accusing them of *fousdari* (violent dacoity, fighting and robbery) and *adaloti* (land disputes). Later the cases were transferred from *upazila* level to district level in Bogra. The group members have so far spent 5000 taka on these cases, mainly to pay bail. The cases are still pending.

After the conflict there were negotiations between the landlords and the members and, after lengthy discussions, a compromise was reached; only three ponds were to be in the hands of the groups, the fourth was to be controlled by the landlords. A verbal agreement was accepted by the members for the time being.

This is typical of the conflicts in rural Bangladesh. Violent clashes over productive resources are common because they involve vested interests preventing the poor from realizing their legal rights to *khas* resources. The image of Bangladesh village society as unchangeable is rapidly cracking. The reasons for conflicts between the rich and the poor are uncountable and cannot be hidden. The conflict is always there but only becomes obvious when the poor organize to claim their legal rights. The groups themselves do not create the conflicts, they merely resist illegal exploitation by the élite. Organization is the poor peoples' best defence against the rich.

Until April 1985, *khas* ponds of less than two acres were leased out by the Union Parishad Chairman, while the ponds of more than two acres were controlled by the UNO at *upazila* level. Since that date all *khas* ponds, irrespective of size, fall under the jurisdiction of the *upazila* chairman. The same goes for *khas* land, which has previously been the domain of *upazila* level officials.

In Shibgonj upazila there are 450 *khas* ponds larger than 2 acres which have been identified by the Proshika workers. The number of ponds of less than two acres is around 1000 and this is in just one of 462 *upazilas* in Bangladesh. In the whole country there are thousands of *khas* ponds, the vast majority of which are unused or more or less destroyed. Most are not controlled by the landless who, according to law, have the right to them. In most cases the landless have no chance of gaining control over *khas* resources, no matter how favourably the law is written.

Through organizing and mobilizing groups, the landless can claim their legal rights in this respect, but they are always opposed by the vested interests of the villages. If all these *khas* resources, government ponds and land, now lying unused or fallow, were turned into productive resources for the landless of Bangladesh not only would there be enormous economic benefits for hundreds of thousands of landless families, but there would also be immense benefits in terms of the national economy.

This step, if realized, would benefit the rural poor more than any number of rural development projects, which experience problems in reaching their target group. Everything necessary to turn ponds into highly productive assets is available locally at low cost. Only the prevailing power structure prevents productive development of these unexploited resources.

In many of the cases where ponds are controlled by landless groups there are readily identified limitations to the efficient use of the ponds. When groups succeed in obtaining a legal lease, it is only for a short period, usually one or three years. This makes it risky for the group to undertake the necessary improvements, such as re-excavation and other labour- or cost-consuming tasks. Also, the vested interests become motivated to mobilize their forces if improvements are made. A re-excavated pond increases in value considerably. Long leases are therefore needed.

If landless groups take control of *khas* ponds by verbal agreement or strength of numbers the problem is the same. Their control is not sufficiently permanent to allow them to risk heavy investments, which means that productivity and therefore their income, is kept at a much lower level than would be possible if their control was secure.

Balorampur Bhumihin Samity, the Landless Society of Balorampur, Shibgonj *upazila*, Bogra Dt, was formed in 1981. There are 18 members in the group who save one taka per head per week and have regular group meetings.

Only three months after the formation of their group, they started fish cultivation in a *khas* pond in the village, which covered 3.21 acres. Floods carried off many of the fish the first year, but the group members were able to catch some which were sold for 2200 taka. However, as in other parts of the country, the pond had formerly been controlled by the rich of the village who claimed their right to the fish. They sent an agent with a net to the pond, to test the reaction of the organized landless. He was caught and his net taken away. He then filed a case against the group members on charges of robbery and assault. The police asked the Union Parishad Chairman to solve the problem without police interference, and it was sorted out in the traditional way by the *shalish* (village court).

In 1982 the landlord group gave bribes of 6000 taka to the Circle Officer and 3000 taka to the CO (Revenue) to obtain an 11 year lease on the pond. When the group members learned about this, they went to the District Fishery Officer, who had not been told about the previous lease. He informed them that the priorities relating to the lease access of *khas* ponds are laid down in law. The first priority is to organized fishermen, the second to the organized landless, the third to social welfare registered co-operatives of the locality, the fourth to Freedom Fighters' Associations and the fifth to women's organized groups. As there was no fishermen's group in the village, the landless had the right to the lease of the pond according to law and the landlord's lease was held to be illegal.

During 1982 the pond was controlled by the *samity*, but as the dispute continued no fish fry were bought and there were no profits that year.

In 1983 the landlords tried to get the lease in the name of a Freedom Fighters' Association. The landless made their application for the lease at the same time. The *upazila* Fishery Officer, after demanding a bribe from the landless without success, decided to give the lease to the party which bid the highest amount. After receiving a bribe from the landlord group he thought better of confronting a well-organized landless group, so asked for a transfer, leaving the troubled waters of Shibgonj in order to go fishing for profit somewhere else!

Normally an annual lease for a pond of this size would be about 300 taka, but as there was competition between the two groups, the rate shot up. Gradually, during the auction, the bids went up to exorbitant rates. The landlords' last bid was 14 800 taka. Although fully understanding the enormous risk of loss, the group members bid another 100 taka and received the lease for 14 900 taka. They had believed it was a three-year lease, but were then informed by the *upazila* officials that it was only for one year. Although everyone was aware that it was far from economically viable, a loan was granted by Proshika because of the importance of getting control over the pond. The group members and the Proshika workers counted on keeping the pond in the hands of the *samity* for years, thereby generating enough incomes to pay back the loan and later to yield a profit for the group.

The group invested 2500 taka in fish fry, but once again floods caused a serious loss and it was barely able to break even.

In 1984 the new chairman, who was in favour of the organized landless, acted as a mediator between the two groups, and argued that there was no point in competition which would only cause further losses for the villagers. He granted a three-year lease for 220 taka to the landless, but when the landlords found out they appealed to the UNO, contending that this arrangement meant a loss for the government, so the UNO cancelled the lease. The landlords' group then offered the chairman 2000 taka for the lease, but he refused it on the ground that it was insufficient compared to the 14 900 taka price of the previous year. The *samity* claimed their legal right to the pond and presented a convincing case to the UNO that the previous year's competition had forced the price unreasonably high. It was finally decided that they would be given a three-year lease for 2200 taka.

During the next season in 1985, there was no flood and the group sold fish with a net profit of 12000 taka. For the coming season they have invested 1200 taka in fry and have calculated profits of 40000 taka if no flood destroys their efforts.

The landlords refused to sit idly by when confronted by a well-organized landless group which had succeeded in claiming its legal rights and proved capable of improving its economic position. Seeking revenge, they fabricated a typical story against the landless group. They took their low lift pump out of its shed and set fire to the shed, then filed a case against the landless group, accusing it of arson, naturally asserting that the pump had been destroyed. This case is still pending, causing expense and trouble for the group, although it is a fairytale from beginning to end.

This is an example of a landless group being well aware of the high economic risks of accepting the lease of a pond at far too high a rate to decide the issue of strength and power between its members and the landlords. It gained a lot of self-confidence by proving that its class, always looked down upon and considered ignorant, is capable of such strength and organization. Through that strength it will be able to keep the pond in its possession, which over the years will mean substantial economic gains.

In Jangram village, Shibgonj *upazila*, Bogra District there are altogether 200 families: 130 are landless and marginal farmers; 50 are small peasants; 15 are rich peasants and 5 are landlords, one is considered big, because he has more than 30 acres of irrigated land, and is successfully running a number of business ventures.

The Jangram Ottor Para Bhumihin Samity, Jangram North Para Landless Society, was formed in 1981. It has 42 members, who have weekly meetings and savings of 1 taka per person weekly. One of the members has received human development training on social mobilization, leadership and organizing from Proshika. On his initiative another three groups were formed within two years, and now they are preparing to form women's organizations too.

By 1982 there were three landless organized groups in the area and they judged themselves strong enough to attempt collective mobilization on the issue of increasing their wages. At that time a day labourer worked 11 hours, from 5 am to 6 pm, for a payment of

10 taka per day plus three meals. Their demand was 20 taka. Finally, after many tough discussions with farmers and landlords and a great deal of tension, they succeeded in getting their claims through.

As labour costs had become more expensive, the landlords put heavy pressure on the organized workers, harassing them during working hours to extort as much labour as possible. As a result the day labourers met to discuss how to achieve an independent stand and reduce the tension and the pressure from the landlords and rich peasants who were buying their labour.

They decided not to sell their labour individually, but instead only to work on a collective contract basis. If any individual was asked to work, he would only accept the whole job, for example to harvest the whole field. The work would then be done by a group of members on a contract basis. This strategy meant two possible gains. Firstly, they could bargain from a stronger position, not as individuals but as a collective, so no pressure could be put on the individual by the landlords. Secondly, they could sometimes raise their wages as high as 40 taka per day when they were working on contract, by settling a flat rate for harvesting a certain field.

At the beginning of 1983 they organized a fourth *samity*, so that nearly every landless or marginal farmer in the village was organized. A village co-ordination committee was formed consisting of four representatives from each of the four groups. They started planning for the reclamation of two *khas* ponds in the village. The ponds were the property of the village but, as often happens, they were controlled by a few of the landlord families.

In April–May 1984, the fishing season before monsoon, the groups took action and went to catch fish in the two ponds. Due to their organizational strength the landlords didn't dare to prevent them, but a village meeting was arranged and the leaders of the co-ordination committee were threatened in their absence by the landlords.

Conspiracies against the group leaders began. The landlords filed a robbery case against two of the co-ordination committee leaders at the *upazila* headquarters. At the same time the landlords arranged a mass-meeting and identified these leaders as 'anti-state elements', conducting underground politics under the cover of *samity* organizing, calling the group leaders criminals and so on. The house of one of the leaders was searched in their efforts to get hold of him for 'special treatment', but he was not at home. The landlords tried their best to terrorize the organized villagers themselves and with the help of the local police.

The village co-ordination committee arranged another meeting to deal with the conspiracy. The leader who had been accused of robbery, went to the *thana* (police station) with some Proshika *kurmis*, claiming that the accusation resulted from the conflict between the different interests of the village, with the result that the Police Inspector asked the Union Parishad Chairman to investigate the case. The chairman organized a meeting between the landlords and the landless, where it became clear that the accusation was false, so it was dismissed. The groups were then granted the lease of the two ponds for three years from the UNO. The two actions made the groups stronger and their recognition in the area was total.

As in all villages, there is a mosque in Jangram, the governing body of which was, naturally, formed by the landlords. Three years earlier there had been a plan to restore the mosque, for which 10000 taka was collected from the village people. Work had been delayed by the governing body for three years, but then the village co-ordination committee, supported by poor peasants and middle peasants, demanded to see the accounts and an investigation of the management of the funds. In a village meeting they proved that the governing body was not acting in the public interest. A new governing body was formed consisting of landless members of the organized groups. They recovered the 10000 taka from the old governing body after a couple of meetings, and the restoration work was done within a short time to everybody's satisfaction.

When groups are well organized and comprise almost all landless and marginal farmers of a locality they can not only claim their economic rights in the form of increased wages but can also become a powerful force in social terms as their strength and unity can make them the leading force in other groups as well, in this example the poor and middle peasants of the village.

Housing

Krishi Bhumihin Shomobay Samity, the Landless Agrico-operative Society of village Sanail, *Singair upazila*, Manikgonj District, was formed two years ago. The 20 members are all from the same village.

On 5 January 1986 they mobilized to take possession of

homestead land for some of their group members. In all there were 56 decimals, out of which 38 decimals were government-owned *khas* land and the remaining 18 vested property. They took possession with the help of all of the organized groups nearby, mobilizing only in their common class interest, rather than for personal gains. The occasion was celebrated by inviting all the organized in the neighbourhood for a meal. A goat was slaughtered and *Milad* was held (traditional prayers in Muslim Bangladesh on occasions such as moving into a new house).

They had obtained the lease from the government without any problems, but after they took possession of the land the local rich people began to raise objections and threatened to take action against the group. The group's reply was that they were prepared for such reactions and they intended to stay, so there was no danger from the talk or threats. The group agreed that five families, who had no homesteads of their own, would settle on the plot. They constructed their bamboo houses with thatched roofs i.e. simple, poor family houses. (According to the civil law of Bangladesh a person who does not have a homestead of his own is allowed to settle on *khas* or vested land and cannot be evicted legally.)

The plot itself was very suitable for use as a homestead. It is on high ground, so there is no risk of flooding. There are a lot of fruit trees and timber trees. It was agreed that the fruits of the old trees would be evenly distributed among all the group members. The new settlers were to plant their own trees and keep the profits from them for themselves.

In this case all the group members acted on behalf of their class, without any view to personal gain. The selection of the five families within the group of 20 who were to settle on this attractive plot went smoothly. There have been no signs of action against the settlements from the rich peoples' quarter so far and the realization of the lease from the government was achieved without problems.

Rice paddies

In Andarmanik village in Harirampur *upazila*, Manikgonj District, there are three landless organizations. The women's group, Andarmanik Anirwan Bhumihin Mohila Samity, has 41 members. The two men's groups, Goalnagor Diapara Bhumihin Samity and

Andarmanik Bhumihin Samity, have 42 and 35 members respectively, bringing the total figure to 118 organized landless. The two men's groups are three years old, while the women's is only two.

Their story concerns the lease of *khas* land of 14 acres, around the River Isamoti, which is silted up and therefore waterfilled only from monsoon until February.

Before 1983 the land was unused but the Goalnagor group began to use the full acreage for *boro* paddy cultivation, without a lease. A good harvest drew the attention of the local vested interests. The group members became aware of the risk of losing the land to the local élite, so they went to acquire a legal lease from the Circle Officer (Revenue) which they obtained quickly and without any problem. Their first harvest was 80 maunds of paddy, nearly 13 000 taka worth.

In 1984 they continued to use the land under lease and planted a new boro crop. Somehow the local rich farmers managed to acquire a double lease on a certain portion of the already leased land by bribing someone at the CO (Revenue) Office. Then at dawn one day they had people cut the paddy which had been planted by the group members on that portion of the land. The group members heard of this and ran to the spot immediately, frightening the people who were cutting the paddy. These then fled to the police station, where they filed a case against the group members on a charge of theft. The group members also filed a suit against the intruders, claiming that they were the legal owners of the whole crop. Ultimately their claim was proved and they won the case.

The 1984 harvest was 100 maunds of paddy, worth 16 000 taka. In 1985 they managed to acquire a legal lease for another two years and were expecting two more good winter crops.

Although the land was legally in the hands of the organized group, the vested interests were powerful enough to keep part of the land and cultivate it and the group was not strong enough to resist. The rich farmers argued that they were entitled to a fair share of the *khas* land, since they were the owners of that land adjacent to the river, which had been eroded. This is another way of claiming land, when you are powerful enough to play tricks for the control of valuable resources.

On the other side of the river was another Proshika-organized group who thought they might enjoy the same income from the river *khas* land as the Goalnagor group had, so they too applied to lease the land. The *upazila* Revenue Officer advised them to occupy the land to succeed in their application.

When the local Proshika *kormis* heard this they intervened and suggested that the two landless groups sit together for discussion, arguing that co-operation and unity among the organized was a must if they were to withstand the local rich. A committee was formed comprising members from both groups, and the women's group, whose involvement was thought to be tactically clever, because they needed numbers to reinforce their strength. In the area both Muslim and Hindu women work in the fields and the groups thought it unlikely that women would be assaulted while tilling the *khas* land. It was agreed that everyone belonging to the local landless class should participate in reaping the crops from the *khas* land.

In 1986 they applied for renewal of the lease in the name of the three *samitys*, but the nearby landowners applied at the same time. The two applications are pending at the time of writing. Although the law clearly states that *khas* land is to be distributed to landless, the nearby landowners are still capable of claiming themselves to be landless with the help of bribes.

The group members have now gained experience. Their strategy is clear; develop the unity and the number of organized in the locality and they will be able to control the river *khas* land forever. They are determined not to allow the vested interests to get hold of the land. The group members have started to become well organized. They are convinced that they will be able to keep the land under their control. What the Revenue Office calls 14 acres of *khas* land is actually more than 20. Altogether there are 60 acres of *khas* land, which is certainly worth fighting for. They now plan to invite more organized groups from the nearby villages to secure control of the whole of the *khas* resource in the future.

In Singar Deghi Gram in Sreepur *upazila*, Gazipur District, there are nine organized groups which were forced to take action against the Forest Department in the area. In 1985, during the monsoon, one of the organized groups paid 350 taka to the local Forest Office for permission to use some 2.5 acres of Forest Department land for one cropping season. This is a common unofficial way of leasing land in forest areas. The payment is made by means of a bribe to the Forest Office staff; the deals are always verbal and there are no documents.

The women's group planted paddy, but one month before harvest, Forest Department staff came to plant saplings on the land. Naturally, the women protested and asked the forest officials to delay the tree-planting for a month until they had cut their paddy. It developed into a conflict. The forester and the ranger came and told the women that is was government land and they were not allowed to use it. The group members replied that they had paid money in personal bribes and would protect their crop until it was time for harvesting.

An official from the Forest Department went to Mabia's house which was on their land and told her that if she took the lead in the protest, they would evict her, but Mabia refused to back down, knowing that she would have the group's support.

Armed guards came from the Forest Department to plant the trees, but around 250 women opposed them, knowing they would hesitate to harm women. A month later the paddy was cut in peace.

The group still has possession of the plot and the Forest Department has not returned. The group is large, well organized and strong. Unity and collective action has paid off.

A marsh

The *haor* (big marsh) is situated in the village Shunsi, in Nagarpur *upazila*, in Tangail District. It is a mile long and half a mile wide and is one of the largest *haors* in the district. It is a deep-water *haor*, so its sole resource is fishing.

Every year it is leased out by the government under open bids in an auction. According to the law, the lease is to be given to the local fishermen's communities, but it is valuable enough to make the implementation of the law slightly elastic. For years the lease has gone to the rich around the marsh, who submit false documents which claim and certify them as fishermen. The usual pattern has then been that they hire the local fishermen, their boats and nets to catch the fish. Thus, instead of legally controlling the *haor*, the catch and the marketing of the fish, the fishermen became day labourers who sold their skills and services to the local elite.

Almost all of the fishermen and landless around the marsh were organized, and in their co-ordination committee meetings they had a lot of discussions about how to get control of the *haor*. They began negotiations with the local élite, claiming their legal right to the incomes from the marsh, but these claims were totally rejected.

Group discussions continued with this experience in mind, and they agreed to take collective action. After the monsoon in 1984 they mobilized all group members around the *haor* and went to catch the fish for themselves.

The local élite responded by filing a loot-case against them. One Proshika *kurmi*, Kuddus, considered to be the leader of the movement was arrested by the police in Nagarpur. On hearing of his arrest, the group members mobilized quickly and formed a procession consisting of 2500 people. They marched towards Nagarpur, chanting slogans about their legal rights and the not-so-legal practices of the vested interests. Outside the *thana* where Kuddus was held, they clashed with the police.

On seeing the size of the procession, the local rich became more interested in negotiations since they realized that they wouldn't be capable of keeping control over the *haor* against that number of organized people. The case was dropped and Kuddus was released. In the negotiations which followed the organized landless were granted 20 per cent of the profits from the *haor* that season, which meant an income of 30000 taka for the groups. This was the first step on the route to final and total control of the marsh resource by the groups.

There was a total of 23 organized groups mobilizing for control or, to start with, a fair share of the *haor*. Nine of them were men's landless groups, six were women's landless *samitys*, two were fishermen's groups, two marginal farmers' groups, three weavers' groups and one carpenters' group.

The following year they stepped up their claims. They had several discussions with the local rich, which culminated in the élite's promising not to bid for the lease in the coming season, on condition that they received 30 per cent of the profits from the catch. The groups would receive 70 per cent.

As there was no competition at the auction, the organized group should have been entitled to a 2-year lease of the *haor* for 31000 taka, but they also had to spend another 135000 taka in bribes. They accepted that this amount was worth paying in view of the size of the resource. The total expenditure of 166000 taka was made up from the 30000 taka profit from the previous year, a loan of 75000 taka from Proshika and their own savings.

They formed a management team consisting of five members from among the 23 groups. This team became responsible for the planning and implementing of the catching and marketing of fish. They hired two guards, a cashier and some clerks for keeping records of the catches and income from sales. The administrative costs were 20000 taka for the first season.

From October 1985 to January 1986 they caught fish to the value of 300000 taka. They calculated another two lakh taka in income before the next monsoon, making their calculated gross income for this first season 0.5 m taka. After their first catch they hoped to repay the Proshika loan easily. All the investments and expenses were covered by this first catch, and they were left with 114000 taka to be shared on the agreed 70–30 per cent basis. With another catch calculated at 200000 taka to be made during the months before the monsoon started this should have turned out to be a very profitable venture indeed.

The group members were fully convinced of their ultimate goal, complete control over the marsh, without any sharing of the income with the local rich. The only feasible way towards this goal was a step by step strategy according to their developing strength. They calculate a probable annual net profit of not less than five lakh taka, to be split among the 23 groups, when the *haor* is in their control, which would imply an average annual income of close to 22000 taka for every group.

Previously, the local élite had the Nagarpur representative in their pockets in the nationwide Bangladesh Fishermen's Society. His cooperation, for which he was of course rewarded, made it possible for the rich to claim part of the fishermen's community, but through their powerful organizational strength the real fishermen now have their own representative in the Bangladesh Fishermen's Society. He is Gopal, a member of Shyampur Landless Rajbongshi Fishermen's Community. No more false documents will now be issued to the rich.

A tubewell

In the village of Barotopa in Sreepur *upazila* in Gazipur District, there are two organized landless groups, Bhai Bhai Bhumihin Samity (the Good Brothers Landless Society) and Bhumihin Darida Samity (the Poor Landless Society). In 1981 they formed one large *samity* consisting of 35 members but two years later they found that the original unit was too big for their meetings and discussions and the members were too scattered, so they split into two groups. There are now 20 and 15 members respectively in the groups, their weekly savings are one taka per person and they have regular meetings every Saturday.

Their first economic project was executed in 1982, when they invested their savings of 2000 taka for sugar-cane cultivation on leased land. The net profit from this venture came to 2200 taka.

In 1983, after the split, the Bhai Bhai Samity borrowed 7000 taka from Proshika and used 500 taka from their own fund to be invested in a sugar-cane crushing machine. Sugar-cane growers came to them to have their crop crushed. (The juice of sugar cane is boiled and put into big earthen jars, where it congeals. This non-refined sugar, *gur*, is the cheapest and the most common sweetening among the rural population.) After two years of sugar-cane crushing the group had repaid the loan to Proshika and were the owners of their own means of production. The profits from the crushing remain intact with the group members.

The experience from the sugar-cane crushing gave them confidence. Economically they were doing well and their deals with the local farmers were well managed. This made them discuss the possibilities of getting into a larger-scale project. They investigated what local resources were available which could be developed and generate income for them.

BADC, Bangladesh Agricultural Development Corporation, had sunk several deep tubewells (DTWs) in the area in 1973. The DTWs were owned by the government, who leased out the irrigation facilities to the farmers at very low rates. The DTWs were managed by local committees dominated by the rich farmers. This was a cheap way of irrigating which was highly subsidized by the government, although in practice the bigger landholders benefited most. The DTW tubewell in Barotopa village had been leased on an annual basis for only 1200 taka by the rich local farmers in 1973.

In the case of Barotopa, as in most of Bangladesh, problems occurred in spite of the extremely good terms offered through these BADC deals, because the management committee failed to achieve a sufficient command area to make performance profitable. The farmers were reluctant to take an active part in the planning and management, as mechanical failures became more and more frequent and the cost of diesel and oil increased. After a couple of years, outstanding debts for the lease were so big that they stopped operating the tubewell.

The group members engaged in lengthy discussions and analysed the reasons for the previous failure of the operation of the DTW. It was a vast local resource lying idle and they were very eager to put their hands on it to operate it themselves.

BADC had begun to sell off their DTWs some years back. For the most part they were bought by the rich farmers and the landlords. CARE, acting as technical advisory body, sinking the tubewells and keeping an eye on their operation and maintenance, had found out from their own and other studies that the utilization and management of the DTWs in the hands of private individuals was far from efficient and optimal and they were enthusiastic when the opportunity to co-operate with Proshika organized landless groups arose. Thus, in 1985, instead of the DTW falling into the hands of one of the local rich farmers, it was agreed that the organized landless of the area would buy it.

The total cost for the procurement of the DTW was 52 000 taka, so the two landless groups decided to act jointly. They received a loan of 92 000 taka from Proshika, of which 52 000 taka was used to buy the DTW from BADC and the remaining 40 000 taka was to cover the operational costs for the first season.

During the first cropping season the tubewell irrigated 18.5 acres, out of which 12 acres were wheat and 6.5 acres were IRRI-paddy (*boro*). The arrangement between the landholders and the groups was that 0.25 of the wheat crop and 0.3 of the paddy crop would be used as payment for the irrigation facilities. As the first season's crops have not yet been harvested, no actual figures can be presented, but the group members calculate that the operational loan of 40 000 taka will be repaid out of the income from this season. Irrigation of 18.5 acres is insufficient to make the best use of the capacity of the tubewell. For the next season the group has negotiated with the landholders of the locality to irrigate around 50 acres. This is essential to make the operation economically viable and profitable.

The main expenses of the first year have been fuel and paying the group members' wages for building irrigation canals. These costs will decrease over time as the irrigation infrastructure is completed and only maintenance is necessary. It is still important to note that irrigation creates a number of job opportunities which benefit the landless labourers.

Although it is a major step forward for the landless to control a means of production this does not mean that their problems are solved. Managing an irrigation scheme brings with it a number of problems and risks, but it is also developing the group's confidence and strength. By a collective effort they have a better chance to solve their problems and manage the project successfully (See Geoffrey D. Wood and Richard Palmer-Jones, *The Water Sellers*, IT Publications 1991).

Vested land

Dhulundi Bhumihin Sramik Samity, the Landless Workers Society of Dhulundi village, in Ghior *upazila* in Manikgonj District, has 50 members. In the village there are two organized groups, one with 44 male members and another with 25 female members. They have regular meetings and group savings.

The Landless Workers Society was formed in January 1982. Only six weeks after their formation, they applied for the lease of an area of vested land just outside the village. The area, 14.82 acres, consists of good cultivable land, a pond and some houses.

The property which had been abandoned by Hindus leaving for India was termed 'enemy property' after the 1965 war between Pakistan and India, when relations between the two countries were tense. When relations improved it was renamed 'evacuee property' and, since the emergence of Bangladesh, it has been termed 'vested property'. It is owned by the government and leased out to tenants with first priority to previous sharecroppers or lessees of the land. If they do not apply for the lease, it is open to anybody.

The members' application was taken care of by the Circle Officer (Revenue), Vested Property Section, Manikgonj, who made a written order to the occupants of the land to surrender it to the government within 7 days and, at the same time, he ordered the Tohsildar Office to recover the land.

At that time the land was occupied by one ex-MP, two advocates (one of them a former Union Parishad Chairman) and another five people, all landlords, prominently led by the ex-MP and the two advocates. The SDO verbally promised the lease to the organized members when the land was vacated. After submitting the application for the lease and receiving this verbal promise from the SDO, the group went and cut the standing crop, paddy, which is the usual way of proceeding in cases like this. Simultaneously the occupants of the land appealed to the higher court in Dhaka to have the SDO order annulled. This case is still pending.

The cutting of the crop in October 1982 took place without any resistance and the group sold the paddy, but then the ex-MP and his advocate companions went into action. They started nine cases against the group. Thirty-four members were accused of theft by one of the landlords; another landlord put the same charge against 24 members. Eight of the landless were anonymously accused of dacoity (armed robbery of buses in the main road at night). Yet another of the landlords accused 24 members of paddy robbery. There was a rape case against five of them based on an accusation by a widow working as a domestic maid servant in the house of one of the landlords. Another case was started against six who cut bamboo on the land and 52 members were accused of robbery of a house in day-time. Two more paddy robbery cases were started against 11 and 9 members, and the latter were also accused of the attempted murder of one of the landlords. This case was filed by a landlord who lived far away and knew nothing about the conflict who had been asked to do so by one of his old friends. The nine cases were all started within three months of the cutting of the crop.

In February 1983 several group members went to plough the land to find that the landlords had organized about 30 people, armed with knives and spears. The fighting resulted in four serious injuries and more than 20 minor injuries.

The society members went to the *thana* and registered a case of attempted murder against the landlords. After two hours of the landlords did the same, bribing the police to arrest and torture seven of the landless, kicking and beating them with bamboo sticks (*lathis*). It is rumoured that the police were paid 12000 taka for this arrest.

The landlords filed a case of attempted murder against 42 members. As the landless had filed a case too, they were convinced that when the police turned up in the village they were coming to investigate their case, but in fact the police had been paid to arrest them. Seven members were arrested and the rest of the organized landless of the village fled and went in hiding for 18 days.

The police dropped the landless case while continuing that of the landlords. Later the SDO reopened the other case of the landless and after 18 days the seven arrested men were let out on bail and the rest of the landless returned from their hide-outs. All 42 accused surrendered to the police with bail petitions. The magistrate decided that six of them would be kept in custody in Manikgonj for 28 days.

The landlords spared no effort to find those who were in hiding. As martial law was in force, the landlords got in touch with an army major from Savar Cantonment, about 25 miles away, and persuaded him to give the local police the authority to move freely in the surrounding seven *upazilas* in their hunt for the forty-two. However, the Proshika Zonal Co-ordinator quickly got in touch with a high-ranking friend within the army, a colonel from Jessore Cantonment, to have the order cancelled.

The two cases of attempted murder which arose at the time of the clash are still pending. The land is again in the landlords' possession and the appeal at Dhaka is still pending. The landless are busy with the cases. Time, police and 'justice' are working in favour of the *status quo*.

The landless have spent 90000 taka on the cases, 40000 for lawyers and the rest for legal deeds, transport etc. They have covered the expenses from their own savings and their collective funds, through contributions from among other group members and from Proshika, and they have taken 21000 taka on loan from villagers. The landlords have spent just as much on legal fees and have had the extra expense of paying bribes. However, they have continued to have useful income from the vested land but they consider the costs involved so far worthwhile, as the plot is valued at at least 15 lakh taka.

The whole process made the Landless Workers Society of Dhulundi village weak. Their organizational experience was too limited for this kind of action only six months after the group was initially formed. Without legal aid and economic support they would have been completely split up and economically ruined. The conflict and the threats made some of the members afraid and hesitant for some time, but now they are having regular weekly meetings again. The plans for collective cultivation of the land are being developed and discussed. They are convinced that they will get hold of the plot when the final appeal from the landlords to take over the legal lease is rejected.

They have endured considerable suffering and expense but they are eager to commence collective farming of the land. Although the process has cost them a great deal, ultimately they are stronger than before and they have become very clear on one point: the need to build their efforts on collective action and the importance of their own strong organization as their only means of reaching their aims.

One Proshika *kurmi* has always stayed very close to the group. He has faced ten cases during this process and is one of those who are still facing the last accusations of attempted murder. His presence has been an important factor in the re-building of the *samity*.

Kolshi Kumuria Prantik Krishi Samity (the Marginal Farmers Society) in Kolshi village, Daulatpur *upazila*, Manikgonj District, was formed in 1982. Initially there were 52 and at present there are 35 members. They all depend on agricultural labour as sharecroppers and land-poor peasants.

In 1977 the future group members already leased 8.13 acres of vested land. The lessees were all the former sharecroppers of the land, and in 1975, when Sheikh Mujib was assassinated, the owner of the land escaped to India. As he was closely connected with the Awami League, he felt insecure. A year later the local Union Parishad Chairman made a resolution to the government, claiming that the land should be declared vested property, as the owner had fled. In 1977 it was declared to be vested by the Circle Officer (Revenue), and the former tillers applied for and received the lease.

In 1979 the group members cut some bamboo on the leased property. But at this time the former owner's son-in-law claimed to be the owner. He filed a case against 25 group members, in collaboration with some rich villagers, accusing them of theft of the bamboo. Four of them were kept in custody while the rest were released on bail by the SDO court in Manikgonj.

At the same time the son-in-law filed a case against the government, claiming to be the heir and legal owner of the land. He maintained that the government declaration that the land was vested was an illegal act. He lost both cases, but filed an appeal regarding the legal ownership of the land to the Commissioner's Court at Dhaka.

By this time two well-to-do Muslims of the area claimed that they had bought the land from the original owner, in a case before the same Commissioner's Court. The case fell to be decided between the two Muslims and the former sharecroppers who were now legally leasing the land and who by this time had formed their *samity*.

When the two Muslims found that the tillers were becoming stronger as they organized, they filed a new case against them, accusing them of theft and dacoity. The police were bribed by the two Muslims and they searched and harassed the group members.

The group members tried a new tactic. They started a petition in their favour among all sections of the people in the union. They received tremendous local support and won the cases, with expenses of 8000 taka in the bamboo theft case and 10000 taka in the dacoity case.

The group was in its infancy, when it ran into these problems. The police harassment and heavy economic burden in connection with the cases, disorganized the *samity* and only 12 members stayed on in the group. It seemed that the ambition of the rich to split them and keep them weak had been successful, but when they won the dacoity case, they started regaining solidarity and the number of members increased again. They managed to cover the huge costs of conducting the cases by selling crops from the leased land. They also sold some of their private cattle to raise as much money as they could among themselves. The leased land had been under their control all the time, and was their main source of social and economic strength.

The members admit that they have benefited from their struggle. 'We did learn a lot. Our organization was new, we were inexperienced. Now we know more and can act maturely, when the time arises. We have gained in experience and organizational strength,' they explain. The group has a legal lease of the land and has always had income from it. They are better organized and have full local support. The only appeal still pending is the original one against the government's declaration that the land is vested property.

Resistance to exploitation by the rich

Village touts

In the village of Kewa Porbekondo, the eastern part of Kewa village, in Sreepur *upazila*, Gazipur District, there are 11 organized groups with 300 members, and three women's groups. A village co-ordination committee has been formed to represent the 11 groups. The organizing work started in 1982 and at first the groups were formed by people from the nearby area. These members formed more groups in their neighbourhood. After some time they also gained the support of Proshika *kurmis*.

During Proshika-organized training at the Area Development Centre at Sreepur, some of the group members participated and fully grasped the complete meaning of their social and legal rights. When they had become strong enough, with 1000 members in the locality, they started taking action.

In April 1985 they mobilized collectively to take back 48 decimals of land which had been held in the possession of one Ahmed Dalal (meaning Ahmed the broker of the village). He had occupied it illegally for 15 years while the real owner of the land, one of the group members, Halim Uddin, had not been strong enough to claim it. All social levels of the village expressed support for the rights of Halim Uddin, but all negotiations failed because Ahmed Dalal was a powerful man. As many of the social conflicts faced by the group members are centered around him, it is worth examining Dalal in more detail.

Some 20 years ago he was an ordinary labourer working in the fields on contract. When Dhaka city started expanding, a lot of better-off people in the surrounding areas of Joydepur, Tongi and Savar invested money in land in the outskirts of the city; land which later became a very profitable source of income as the demand for industrial plots and for housing expanded rapidly. Ahmed Dalal started acting as a broker between sellers and buyers of land, building a new career and making some money. After a couple of years in this business he had developed enough skills to procure false landholding documents, i.e., stealing land in a way which is all too common in Bangladesh. Soon he became a low-level *matbar* (village headman), further developing his capabilities of cheating and acting shrewdly to his own advantage. To start with he possessed less than an acre of land on his own, but, mostly through illegal means, he has occupied another 8–9 acres over the years. He has been married five times. His first wife was found hanged, his second was poisoned. Now he lives with three wives and has seven sons and eight daughters. His history is quite a typical one — a man working himself up from marginal farmers' status, by more or less criminal methods, to a position of relative wealth and power, often with many wives and children, who acts very strongly and speaks out against his old class, the landless and marginal farmers.

All negotiations with Ahmed Dalal failed. At this point the group members approached the UNO, showing him all the documents and explaining the criminal acts of Ahmed Dalal. The UNO issued a notice for Ahmed Dalal to appear before him and asked him either to surrender the land to the legal owner or immediately produce a receipt from Halim Uddin. Ahmed Dalal now tried to persuade the group members and Halim Uddin to sell the plot to him as it was situated close to his house. Negotiations started, an amount was agreed upon and a contract was signed. Dalal then went with this contract to the UNO, to prove that they had reached a deal. Halim Uddin received no money for the plot. The group settled a date for collective action. In large numbers they went to the plot and cut the standing crop of sugar cane.

Ahmed Dalal filed a case against 12 of the group members, accusing them of theft and two of them were arrested. When this news spread, some 600 group members assembled at the police station to protest but because it was night, the two arrested were not released on bail until the next morning. The people went home after taking a decision for a social boycott of Ahmed Dalal.

The social boycott succeeded. No one would work for him in the fields, no rickshaw would take him and local buses refused to take him. The boycott is still going on. He was compelled to work in his fields himself together with his sons, as the boycott foiled his efforts to give the land out on a sharecropping basis. Finally he was forced to leave his village home and stay with relatives in the *upazila* headquarters.

The land dispute went to the court, and the verdict was that the plot belonged to Halim Uddin. The case against the 12 group members was therefore dropped, as they could hardly be accused of stealing a crop under the orders of the legal owner.

On the same day as the labourers had mobilized to cut the sugar cane, they also erected a hut on a one-acre plot belonging to another group member, Adbul Mannan. He was landless and had received the plot for permanent settlement from the government some three years before, but the land had been forcibly occupied by Ahmed Dalal, who sent his people to destroy the hut. The group members went once again to the UNO, who came to the spot together with the magistrate and the settlement officer from the Officer Land Administration Department, who is record-keeper of *khas* land. They directed the group members to reconstruct the hut. Two days later Ahmed Dalal had it set on fire. The Village Defence Party and the police on patrol caught one of the sons of Ahmed Dalal red-handed and he was arrested together with two of his brothers and Ahmed Dalal himself. They spent 11 days in Dhaka Central Jail before being released on bail.

Ahmed Dalal had by now been severely rebuffed. His pride was badly hurt and he had lost his social prestige. To avenge himself he filed a new case against the same 12 group members, accusing them of looting and plundering the house of his son-in-law. He claimed that valuables worth 40000 taka had been taken, but even his own relatives had had enough of him. The son-in-law's own father explained in the court that the whole story was nothing but a fabrication and the case was withdrawn. The group members then claimed compensation, for the expenses they had incurred in connection with the false case. A spontaneous *shalish* (village arbitration) was held and he was ordered to pay 2000 taka. He then made a public apology and paid 1000 taka, at which the group members expressed their satisfaction, since his apology in public was worth more than any money.

From a social point of view these examples from among the organized landless of Kewa are very important. Through their numbers, unity, consciousness and ability to achieve a broad mobilization, they have made tremendous social gains. They have shown that it is possible for the poor to tackle the dominance and illegal activities of a powerful village tout. United, the landless become a power to count on. They will never more accept the kind of exploitation that Ahmed Dalal so successfully demonstrated before. They have now the tools for fighting back. Consciousness, unity, experience and a great number of members organized, all knowing what mobilization for their rights means.

Jiten Samaj Kallyan Samity (Jiten Welfare Society) Bonagram village, in Mukshudpur *upazila*, Gopalgonj District, was formed two years ago. Jiten was the name of a group member who died, and in recognition of his services, the group was named after him. There are 40 members, they have monthly meetings and save five taka per member every month. Catching and selling fish is the main occupation of all the group members. They have all developed their social consciousness to a high degree through discussion and training.

On 17 January 1985 they faced a grave social issue. It was the time for the annual Ganga Puja, one of the major Hindu festivals for communities of fishermen. One of the union members, named Hero-member, demanded 1000 taka from one of the group members, Niranjan, who was also the leader of the local *puja* committee. Hero-member claimed that all the other *puja* committees of the locality, who were all from poor, low-caste fishermen *paras*, had paid him 5–700 taka, so the demand of 1000 taka should be considered a good bargain.

The tradition of extracting money at celebrations has been going on for decades. It was a common feature even in the old days of the Raj, when *zamindars* used to do the extracting. Today the tradition is kept alive by the local élites who use the money to have a good time. What Hero-member was demanding from the poor of the community was money needed for food and drink for himself and his friends during the Ganga Puja nights. Although drinking is prohibited for Muslims, Hero-member was happy to ask for money to drink in public.

Hero had started his career as a Razakar, a member of the pro-Pakistan anti-Liberation para-military organization. After Liberation he became an ordinary dacoit with good connections with a number of criminal gangs in the Faridpur area. As a successful dacoit, he had also developed a very good understanding with and co-operation from the law enforcement agencies. During the previous Union Parishad elections, Hero had wanted to run for the position of representative of the people and the local police were very helpful, moving him around in the villages during the campaign and asking the villages to vote for him. With this heavy support from the police, Hero was of course declared elected and became Hero-member, exploiting new ways of developing his career.

The group had taken a decision to put a stop to the extortion, so Niranjan, the group member and *puja* committee leader, told Hero-member that they would not pay, saying '*Boro kota, chotto mukh*' ('big words from a small mouth'). Hero-member promised to teach him a lesson for this behaviour.

The same evening Hero-member returned to the village and, heavily drunk, he destroyed parts of the *puja* house and some 15 of the simple dwelling houses of the fishermen families. He abused Niranjan in strong language, but as Niranjan was away at the Proshika office, the climax of the lesson, the beating, had to be postponed.

Next morning Niranjan went to the market place with his Proshika friends. Hero-member appeared and hit Niranjan but, before anything severe developed, the people around interfered to put an end to the attack. Hero-member claimed the matter was none of their business, but just between him and Niranjan.

This news spread quickly, as is usual in a market place. When they heard, some 70–80 group members who were in the bazaar chased Hero-member and his companions away. He took refuge in a house, which was surrounded by the group members and some other people from the market place. The social élite arrived and tried to calm things down. They suggested a *shalish* to solve the conflict peacefully. The group members agreed, as their only demand was justice, and started leaving the house to return to the market place. Then, suddenly, they were attacked from behind by some of Hero-member's friends. Four or five of them were heavily beaten; one, Umar Ali, received a severe injury to the back of his head and was hospitalized for two weeks.

The situation had now changed. The group members who had agreed on peaceful arbitration had been beset by violence at their backs. The same afternoon the members of more than 20 organized groups assembled to discuss a joint campaign. As they didn't want their discussions to leak out, they decided to spend the afternoon spreading the news to other groups and to have another meeting indoors that evening. Some 250 members participated in the meeting and decided to take revenge. They decided to answer violence with violence.

The next morning 5000 villagers, equipped with 2000 bamboo or cane screens for protection and armed with spears and *ramdao* (a kind of machete) marched towards Hero-member's house near the market place. They were stopped by Proshika workers, who argued that they had chosen a dangerous strategy. Five thousand armed men could provoke any situation at the bazaar. Their enemies, the vested interests and Hero-member's friends, would most probably use the occasion to their advantage, laying the blame for any looting and plundering of shops or violence towards women on the organized. The Proshika *kurmis* suggested that they not enter the market place. Seven social leaders, one ex-chairman and one present chairman and some members, proposed that they should act as mediators. They promised to have a *shalish* organized within a few days, where they would guarantee a just settlement of the conflict.

The *shalish* was never held because Hero-member was too scared to leave his house. He was sure he would be killed, as soon as he showed himself, although the arbitrators assured him that nothing would happen.

A few weeks later Hero-member made a written apology to Niranjan, but he wouldn't accept it, because all the organized in the locality were involved. After a little while when feelings on the issue were cooling down, Hero-member forwarded another apology, which was eventually accepted.

Finally, it was Hero-member who learned a lesson. He has become friends with Niranjan, and has since acted very positively towards the organized poor of the area and towards Proshika. The united mobilization of the organized of the locality turned out to be overwhelming. Not even the powerful Hero-member could remain untouched, when his actions made 5000 organized men march towards his house. The group members showed that united and mobilized in an action of class solidarity, they are definitely a powerful force.

The old tradition of extracting money at the times of *puja* has come to an end. Last year there were no such attempts whatsoever during the Ganga Puja, thus one of many traditions of exploitation came to an end through the initial action of the Jiten Samity of Bonagram village.

False claims for religious purposes

In Barotopa village, Sreepur *upazila*, Gazipur District, there are three organized women's groups. The members of Mayer Achal (Motherly Affection), Chalarpath (Way of Starting) and Bacherpath (Way of Living) have been organized for four years. Altogether there are 48 group members, who have weekly meetings and save one taka per person per week. Their savings have mainly been put into collectively owned cows.

At the time of the Korbani Eid, when the Muslims are sacrificing cattle and having big feasts, the Islamic religion says that the sacrificed cattle are to be divided into three even parts. One third is for the owner and his family and the remaining two thirds are to be given away, without condition, one third to be distributed to nearby relatives who cannot afford to sacrifice and the last third to be given to the poor in the neighbourhood. If any conditions are given in connection with the distribution the religious principle is broken and the sacrifice is invalid.

At Korbani in 1984 when cattle were sacrificed in Barotopa, the élite of the village said that unless a payment of 20 taka was made by every poor family of the village, no share of their third of the meat would be distributed. The money collected was to be given to the imam of the local mosque as payment for his religious services.

The members of the three women's groups under the leadership of Zamela Khatun protested. According to Muslim ethics they were entitled to their third because they were poor and it was against the spirit of the Holy Koran to ask for money. Finally they refused to take their shares under these conditions and left. Later they were asked to come back for negotiations. They all sat down and discussed how much they could afford and their contribution was set at 6 taka per family. They then took their shares to the Korbani sacrifice, as their claims had been successfully met.

The next year the élite had learned their lesson. There were no conditions made to the poor for their share of the Korbani sacrifice. They were cordially invited to contribute to the imam if they could afford to do so, but this was never a precondition of the Korbani sharing.

A fraudulent sharecropper

Another story involving the organized women of Barotopa village claiming their rights concerns a member of one of the groups who had a small plot of land covering about a third of an acre. Her husband was ill and had no means of cultivating it himself, so the plot was sharecropped by another man from the village. The deal was the most common, fifty-fifty to be shared between the sharecropper and the owner with the sharecropper doing all the work.

The sharecropper planted jute on the plot. Then without informing the owner, he cut the crop and took all of it for himself. When the owner's wife found that the jute had been cut in her absence, she went to the sharecropper's house for her share, but he offered her only 1.5 maunds of jute, which clearly enough was less than half the harvest. She claimed that the cash equivalent of 2.5 maunds was a reasonable 50 per cent share but he refused to accept this, and made no payment at all, thinking that he was dealing with a weak woman.

Finding no alternative she and the rest of her group members went to his house. Seeing many women approaching his house, the sharecropper fled. As he appeared not to be interested in negotiating, they used other means to claim their members' rights and took one of his goats.

The wife kept the goat for two weeks. Although the sharecropper sent people to reclaim it, promising that the accurate amount would be paid within a few days, she kept it until he paid the full amount of 300 taka, equivalent to the value of 2.5 maunds of D-class jute, 120 taka/maund.

Women fight for their rights

The life of Amena Begum; from misery to dignity

Exploitation is an everyday fact. The differences between the rich and the poor are vast. These simple facts are often disguised by a policy of treating the poor as something non-human. This simplifies the good lives of the rich. Sayings like 'All men have an equal right to live' are useful at decent occasions and celebrations, but in practice it is easier not to see the perpetual inequalities. It is most convenient to stay silent. Silence means security for those who want to maintain the *status quo*. The sufferings of 'non-humans' become bearable for the privileged, and they can always be dealt with by petty alms or relief from their 'superiors'. Of course, it is not relief or alms that the poor actually need, it is support in their struggle for equality and their right to human dignity, for a society organized in such a way that everybody has the opportunity to lead a decent life and where there is work, food, education, health care and basic security for all.

Amena Sardar is a widow, about 40 years of age, whose husband died eight years ago. As she was the chair of Khodal Dhara Mohila Samity, the Mattock-working Women's Society, in Nagarpur *upazila*, Tangail District, we asked her to tell us her story.

Amena explained that her past was so unhappy that she did not want to tell very much about it, but some fragments will provide a clear enough picture.

She was married at the age of ten to a poor young agricultural labourer. At that time the dowry system only applied to the very rich. It was rather the opposite amongst the poor; the father of the bridegroom paid Amena's father 100 taka 'bride's price' which, taking account of inflation, would be equal to 5000 taka today.

Their marriage consisted entirely of sorrow and misery. During these years she gave birth to nine children, three of whom died early, and at the time of her husband's death she was five months pregnant. Today she has three sons and three daughters, the first son and two of the daughters being married. The little land they had, including the homestead, had to be sold to obtain money for the treatment of the liver trouble which caused her husband's death. They had no food for the children, no house to live in and no clothes to wear. After the birth of her ninth child, Amena had nothing to put on except ragged jute cloth.

She then had to carry the responsibility for bringing up six children on her own. She went to get a job as an earth-worker, to earn money to feed the children, but nobody would hire her, as they thought her children would hamper her work. She gave the smallest child to a relative because she couldn't look after him while doing heavy work. Four of the other five children, one son and three daughters, were placed in the houses of different people in the nearby villages to serve as domestic labourers with no salary, only for food and shelter. Only the remaining son stayed with her.

She started selling her labour in earthcutting schemes to survive. When harvesting was over in the rich farmers' fields, she was allowed to pick up the leftover grains. (This system prevails all over the country and is called *dhan sira* or *kurano*.) Her troubles did not stop when she returned home. The house had been sold during her husband's illness and now the buyer, a rich farmer, pressured her to leave it. Ill treatment and harshness had become everyday experiences for her.

Her eldest daughter returned to live with her, and they worked together with the earthcutting, which improved their earnings. They had three meals a day and earned 3–4 taka per head from the work. They started saving money to buy back the house.

At that time a young man turned up at their working site and enquired about their wages, working hours and living conditions. He would come more or less every day, sitting down for informal talks. After some time he proposed that they form a *samity*, to unite and organize to fight for higher wages and against the exploitation in their everyday lives.

Amena and the rest of the labourers were very suspicious that he would want a fee from them, but as time passed and nothing of that was said their suspicions faded and they agreed to form an organization. The group consisted of 80 women and they started saving 5 taka per person each month. Amena took the chair and another strong woman became the cashier of the *samity*. However, as their savings totalled 400 taka each month, the members still strongly suspected that the young man would make financial demands any day and the cashier was strictly forbidden to hand over any money without prior approval from the members. The months went by, and the young man said nothing about money; rather, by his advice and their own unity, they managed to raise their daily wages from 3 to 5 taka. Their suspicions disappeared and they came to know the young man as Haroon bhai, the Proshika *kormi*, and their close friend.

Amena and the three other members went for human development and social analysis training at the Proshika ADC in Nagarpur. Through the training they began to understand the nature of the society they were living in. 'This made it possible to measure the society and its social system through the bitter experiences of my life,' Amena explained. 'I was able to change my life through our organization.' Soon after the training she went to the rich families which were keeping her children as domestic labourers and succeeded in obtaining a cash salary for them in addition to their food.

Later, from her own savings and wage increases, she regained her 12-decimal homestead land for 1300 taka. Using her own savings and those of her two eldest sons, the three of them constructed three tin sheds with bamboo fencing, one for the now married eldest son, another for the second son and a third for herself and the youngest son. They have become virtually self-reliant. 'Once the children and myself were totally uprooted. By our own efforts we have managed a real home,' she says.

Today she is engaged as a supervisor for road maintenance and receives a monthly salary of 360 taka. She is one of 15 female members of the Coordination Committee of the Nagarpur area and is highly respected by her fellow organized women. 'Once I could part from my sons and daughters, but parting from the unity and solidarity of the *samity* would be impossible,' she explains, 'The group, the *samity*, has become a part and parcel of my life. Through organizing together, our lives have developed from inferiority and uselessness into unity, strength and reliance on each other in our fight for a worthy future for our children.'

Women against divorce

Shingaspur Modhupara Bhumihin Mohila Samity, the Shingaspur Middle Para Landless Women Society, in Shibgonj *upazila*, Bogra District, was formed two years ago. The group has 11 members and holds weekly meetings. Their savings, 2225 taka, have been invested in a collectively owned cow. Two of the members have received 'Women and development' training at the Proshika ADC in Shibgonj.

The husband of two of the members once had his clothes stolen while they were drying after having been washed. He got very angry with his two wives, and he said that they didn't take proper care of the clothes. His anger resulted in his divorcing his first wife at the local Marriage Register Office.

His elder brother's wife, who was a member of the *samity*, came to know about the divorce and the reasons behind it. The divorced wife stayed in her house while the other members, including the second wife, were contacted. When the husband tried to evict the first wife out from the house, the group members opposed him and compelled him to remarry her. This took place within five days, according to the Muslim practice.

By their action, the first wives of the two brothers and the group prevented a *hilla* marriage. This form of divorce is not recommended by law, but is still practised in many parts of rural Bangladesh. Often it is referred to as Muslim law and is described as punishment of a husband. When a husband has divorced a wife, she is forced to spend a minimum of two days and two nights with another man, although this period may vary from two days to three months according to the practice in different localities. The idea is that if she remarries before him, he can then remarry himself. Her forced stay with another man is considered as her remarriage.

Although it is called a punishment of the husband, this indicates a form of severe male chauvinism as it is in fact the former wife who is directed to spend time with a man who, under normal circumstances is selected by her ex-husband, the man who has just divorced her!

The story illustrates a situation where women banded together to further their rights and dignity as women in a situation which is traditionally governed by men. Perhaps the member who deserves the most recognition is the second wife who supported her traditional enemy, the first wife.

In Singar Deghi Gram, in Sreepur *upazila*, Gazipur District, nine women's groups were formed three years ago, with a total membership of 139 organized women. The nine *samitys* are:

o Uzzol Samity No. 1 (The Bright Society No. 1);

- Uzzol Samity No. 2 (The Bright Society No. 2);
- Goriber Ekkota (Unity of the Poor);
- Aderer Alo (The Light of the Dark);
- Bacherpath (The Way of Existence);
- Ashar Alo (The Hope of the Light);
- Mayer Achal (Motherly Affection);
- Bhumihin Ekkota Samity (The Landless Unity Association);
- Kazol Samity (The Beauty of the Eye Association).

The chair of the village co-ordination committee covering the nine groups is held by Mabia Khatun who is also cashier of Uzzol Samity No. 1. She is an outspoken woman, expressing her disgust towards the rich class of the society, who exploit the poor in different ways. She tells about the group members' efforts to deal with the effects of the exploitation.

In August 1985, 37 female members under the Proshika ADC in Sreepur were sent to Koitta, the Proshika central training unit outside Manikgonj, for training in silkworm breeding. Six of these women came from the nine *samitys*. The training was aimed at giving the women a possibility to earn money for their families' welfare through rearing silkworms on their homesteads. A popular theatre performance was staged by the members of the groups describing what happened.

The rich of the local society did not like the women going for training and claimed that it was against their religion. They objected to the whole idea of women sitting together having meetings, discussions and co-operation with organized groups of men. The *matbars* (village social leaders) considered it to be disobedience towards Muslim values, so they put pressure on the women's husbands while they were away. They urged the husbands to take serious religious action against their wives, which means that they were actually encouraging the husbands to divorce their wives. If anybody failed to take action, the *matbars* threatened that they would ensure that he would not have job opportunities or support in the future. They even threatened to have the families turned out of the village.

One of the husbands was forced to divorce his wife after 20 years of happy marriage. At this, the rest of the group members reacted strongly and questioned the husband who explained that he had not acted of his own free will, but under duress. The women pointed out that the Muslim religion does not permit an act like divorce to be forced and asked him to take his wife back, which he happily did.

The group members then staged their drama, focusing on how the poor wives could be forced to divorce by the social élites. After divorce, the women are in the hands of the social élite, on whom they depend for employment. When this happens they are totally without any rights and are very often sexually used by the men in the rich families of the village. The drama also seriously criticized the stand of the *matbars*. This was a brave thing for women from poor households to do. Mabia Khatun herself played the role of the divorced woman.

The élite were furious and picked out Mabia as the target for their anger, by depriving her of her tiny plot of land, but with the help of the rest of the women, she regained it after a couple of months. At the moment relations are good and the tension is over, but there will be no more forced divorce in the village.

An unregistered marriage

In the village of Gadar Bhajandi in Mukshudpur *upazila* in Gopalgonj District, a marginal women farmers' group with 18 members was formed one and a half years ago. Called Paruly Women's Society after one of the group members, they hold bi-monthly meetings and their savings are 10 taka per member each month. Two of the group members have gone through human development training at the Proshika ADC in Mukshudpur. There are three other women's groups and two men's groups in the village.

The actions of this women's group were able to resolve a social injustice which arose out of an unregistered marriage of a young girl in their locality.

The girl, Begum, was 15 or 16 years old. She couldn't continue her studies after fifth class, as her family was too poor to keep her at school. Her family needed income, so when an opportunity arose for her to receive training in bee-keeping, she and some other young girls from the area took it up. The training was given close to the nearby bazaar.

A man, Chand Mia who had quarrelled with his wife, had rented a house in the bazaar. He was a deed writer and earned quite a good living from his work at the local Sub Registry Office. He had been married 12 years and was the father of six children. He saw Begum at her training sessions and was attracted by her beauty and youthfulness. He took steps to become acquainted with her family. As a professional deed writer, he knew how to deal with affairs of this kind tactfully and moved gradually and very carefully, using Begum's family's poverty as a weapon in his design. He learnt everything about their economic problems and lent them small amounts now and then, thus becoming a part of the family.

When the situation had developed favourably enough for him, Chand Mia told Begum's parents that he wished to marry her. The poverty-stricken family could not easily refuse someone who had been so helpful towards them, so they thought over the proposal. Chand Mia's income was quite good. He had land as well as the income from his profession and his offer seemed to imply security for Begum and a chance for the poor family to improve their conditions slightly, so they overlooked that fact that he was 40 years old and already supporting a wife and six children. They agreed to his proposal without looking too deeply into his personal circumstances.

Chand Mia then explained that his brother-in-law had borrowed 30 000 taka from him and would refuse to pay back the loan if he came to know about this second marriage. He therefore proposed that the marriage should not be registered according to the Bangladesh law. Begum's parents were in his hands. They could not refuse his proposal, for fear that their daughter's own security would suffer if he did not receive the 30 000 taka, so the marriage was settled in accordance with Islamic customs but without legal registration, but this was not known in the village.

Chand Mia visited his new wife every night, arriving late at night and leaving at day-break. This continued for a couple of months. Begum soon fell pregnant and requested her husband to take her to her father-in-law's house, according to the usual practice, but Chand Mia always had excuses for not doing so.

Gradually the news of the marriage spread over the area, but Chand Mia's visits to his wife became less frequent and soon stopped completely. Begum, expecting his child, sent for him, but he now denied the marriage.

The members of the Paruly Mohila Samity considered this to be a serious crime and a severe social injustice towards Begum. Chand Mia had used the family's poverty to satisfy his lust. The *samity* contacted the other group in the village and had a meeting with the local élites. Soon public feeling was aroused and the group members pressed for a public meeting with Chand Mia and his father. When the situation was explained to him, Chand Mia's father took Begum to his house, as is the custom. It began to look as if the problem was solved.

But at her father-in-law's house a new chapter started in Begum's life. Humiliation, physical torture and harassments became part of her daily existence. Chand Mia's first wife and her brother made life unbearable for Begum and when she could tolerate it no longer, she took refuge in her parents' house.

The group members raised funds among themselves to send Begum to the Zonal Marital Law Court in Jessore to tell the story of her marriage and maltreatment. The court ordered the arrest of Chand Mia's father and the first wife's brother although they were later released on bail.

The *upazila* chairman was asked to act as a mediator. When he asked Begum if she had anything to prove her marriage with Chand Mia, she could not produce proof on paper, but she could show a palm-leaf fan, which she had used to fan her husband with. On it Chand Mia had written his name and address along with Begum's name. Everyone who knew Chand Mia could easily recognize his handwriting so Chand Mia could no longer deny his connection with Begum. Moreover the boatman, who had been paid by Chand Mia to ferry him over to Begum's family house to visit her, appeared as a witness and recounted the frequent journeys in front of hundreds of people who had gathered. Chand Mia's guilt was clear enough. The crowd expressed their disgust over his base exploitation of a poor family. He was ordered to take responsibility for Begum and her child and the marriage was formally registered in the Mukshudpur *upazila* court. For concealing the facts of his second marriage, he was fined 25000 taka, which was to be kept on fixed deposit in Begum's name.

Since that time Begum has been staying with her husband at his house and there have been no problems between her and the first wife or her brother. Now and then she visits her parents' house, expressing content with her life. Unfortunately her baby, born prematurely, died, but she has recovered and is once again happy with life.

The members of the Paruly Mohila Samity proved to be an

effective force even though they had only been organized for a year. They had mobilized for the cause of justice for a woman who was not a member of their *samity* or any other organized group. Their action in mobilizing and motivating the other local people made it possible to achieve justice and have Chand Mia's misdeeds publicly revealed and they gave financial support for Begum's legal proceedings at the court in far-away Jessore. Their awareness, in combination with the mobilization of the consciousness of the other villagers, and their readiness to offer financial support, made the quest for justice successful.

Dignity and dowry

In Charjamalpur village, in Singair *upazila*, Manikgonj District, there are five Bhumihin Mohila Samity (Landless Women Societies) which were formed three years ago and comprise a total of 98 women. Most of the members are engaged in earthcutting work in Food for Work schemes or as labourers in brickfields.

Alea Begum (Alea means Lightgiver) holds the chair of the co-ordination committee of the five groups. She says that she has become fully aware of the exploitation patterns of the local élite and how poor people were suppressed by social rules and patterns, while receiving training on social analysis at the Proshika ADC in Singair. After the training, in which a number of group members participated, the co-ordinating committee agreed to pay special attention to unfair wages and social issues.

At this time there was an incident when a village man cut the straw in a paddy field belonging to a group member for use as fodder. The woman saw the man taking away the straw and ran to him, protesting. The man went to one of the representatives of the social élite in the village, complaining about the woman's daring and rude behaviour towards him. The complaint was forwarded to her husband's elder brother and he threatened to beat her in public for lack of respect towards a man. Her husband, furious at her behaviour, expelled her from their house.

The members gathered to explain to the husband that his wife had been acting in his interest in protecting their property. The husband understood, apologized to his wife and asked his elder brother to make an apology too. The brother made a public apology. Thus the women succeeded in claiming fair treatment and received apologies for mistakes made by two men who were backed by attitudes of the social élite.

Sometime afterwards a group of women was engaged in earthcutting work at a road construction site in a government *upazila*-level scheme. At this site they were working for money rather than under the more common Food for Work. It was agreed that, on completion of the work, the women would receive a total of 300 taka to be split among them. During construction they received only 100 taka; the rest was to be paid when the work was completed.

Working without daily payment created big problems for the women who needed the money to be able to buy food for themselves and their families. They put forward this claim and, the next day, protested by stopping work. A supervisor from the *upazila* arrived, and they explained why they were claiming daily wages. He seemed understanding but explained that if they were paid daily, they might leave the earthcutting work before it was completed, since it was winter and there was better-paid work elsewhere. The women insisted that they would not do this and from the next day they were paid on a daily basis.

The groups also had thorough discussions on the problems of dowry, asking who gained by the system and where had it come from. The older women knew that it had been adopted from the practice of the rich, who could afford it. Among the poor it only created huge problems. It was a very common reason for borrowing money at exorbitant interest rates from the local *mahajan* (moneylender). The debts often forced them to sell their last plots of land to the *mahajan* at low rates. The older women told the younger ones that when they were young, the system had been the opposite. At that time the bride and her family received gifts or money at the marriage ceremony.

They decided to act by agreeing that when it was time for marriage for their sons and daughters, they would neither take nor give dowry. Very soon they had marriage ceremonies of a new kind in the village. Three daughters of group members married boys from outside the groups' families and a group member's son was married to the daughter of another group member without dowry. These marriages have generated great interest in the area and other poor people have reacted positively.

'The rich have money. We have the strength of our unity. With this unity we are facing them, their power and their imposed manners and social patterns,' concluded Alea the Lightgiver.

Literacy

Paschimkalimpur Anirban Mohilar Samity (the Lighted Lamp Women's Society) of West Kolilpur, Harirampur *upazila*, Manikgonj District, was formed two years ago. It has 16 members who have bi-monthly meetings and save five taka per person each month.

Their main objectives in forming the group were to enable themselves to resist social injustice, multiple marriages, divorce, assault, humiliation and dowry. They had to be united (*ekkota*, literally 'saying the same word') because they wanted to take action to increase their labour wage and to establish their sharecropping rights.

They started their own literacy training for two main reasons. Firstly they had had bad experiences of being cheated by people buying their labour because they could not read. They had received five seers of wheat as payment for certain work and then put their thumb prints on papers which stated that they had received 15 seers. Secondly they wanted to learn basic accounting, reading and writing to be able to run and control the *samity* on their own.

They identified their own need for literacy training; it was never suggested by the Proshika *kurmis*. Most of the members are working as earthmovers at government schemes under Food for Work. At every work site there is supposed to be a signboard explaining the basic facts about the project: who the members of the project committee are, what amount of wheat has been allotted and the payment per 1000 cubic feet of earth moved. They certainly needed to be able to read this.

Two of the 16 members of the group can read and write, Rohima Khatun, the chair, and one other. These two have taken responsibility for imparting their knowledge to the rest of the members.

They use leaves from the palmyra instead of expensive paper, make their pens out of the thin branches of bamboo and produce permanent ink from the juice of the leaves of beans or corolla. All these things are freely available in the village.

During the week, between classes, they try their best to practise on their own at home, writing with a piece of charcoal on the floor while they do the cooking, or on the ground outside their houses.

They started five months ago, and now everybody can write her own name and they have just started easy reading and making sentences.

Their ambition is to continue learning until all of them know enough to be able to read and write letters to local government offices and to distant relatives, up to the point where anyone in the group can read and write minutes from their group meetings and handle the accounts. They sit together every Friday for at least two hours while the men go to the local market.

Increasing wages

Food for Work

In Nagarpur *upazila*, Tangail District, an earth road is under construction between Selimpur and Dhupuria. It is covered by a Food for Work scheme, which applies to four miles of road under Selimbad Union. The total wheat allocation for this portion is 1670 maunds (about 6.2 tonnes). There are thousands of schemes like this, mainly during the winter season, all over Bangladesh.

Forty female labourers from four women's groups are involved and 100 male labourers from five male groups. They have all been organized for several years. The wheat allocation per 1000 cubic feet of earth moved from the roadside pits up to the road level is 50 seers (about 46.7kg). Payment is made weekly. Sometimes the payment is delayed for a day or two, but never more.

The labourers work from 6 am to 11 am and on an average day each worker earns five seers of wheat per day. At the initial stage of the scheme the market value of five seers of wheat was 25 taka. When wheat harvesting started, the value dropped to 17–18 taka and reached 11–12 taka later on, when there is a surplus of wheat.

The labourers are satisfied with the employment opportunities created by this kind of project. It is not very well paid, but as the daily working hours are limited to five, they can also be involved in other income-generating activities, although their purchasing capacity decreases heavily as the value of the five seers of wheat declines.

As organized group members they are very much aware of their rights and due shares. They do not face any problems when it comes to fair measurements of allotments.

'If we fail to pay the allotments in due time, the labourers will give us a lot of trouble,' says the supervisor of the scheme. 'They are organized and put heavy pressure on us for fulfilment of our part of the deal. Their working hours are few, but they certainly work hard during these five hours daily. We make the proper measurements and pay the proper payments. In return they do proper work, taking full responsibility without any fuss or shirking.'

Misappropriation and inaccurate payments and measurements are very common in projects such as this. They are so frequent that the government has actually made misappropriation of up to 30 per cent of the total allotment in this type of scheme legal! If the labourers are organized, proper payment and measurement can be achieved without conflict. In return they perform high-quality work and take responsibility for what they are doing so the scheme gains, as well as the labourers.

The women of Boldara union, Singair *upazila*, Manikgonj District, started organizing two and a half years ago. They had one large *samity* consisting of 62 women but it became very difficult to hold meetings, keep the accounts of the collective savings and get all the members together, so they decided to split the large group into three smaller ones in 1985. These are called Anondomoy, which means Joyful, Sudjumoki, meaning Sunflower and Golap, Rose. All of them are Bhumihin Mohila Samitys, Landless Women Societies. They have one village co-ordination chairman for the three groups, Baherjan Bibi. Most of the group members are earthcutting labourers, mainly for road construction under the Food for Work programme.

A year ago 30 members from the three groups worked in such a road construction project. Earthcutting and earthmoving of a specific area and quantity were agreed on to be rewarded with 16 maunds of wheat, but they were given only nine maunds when the work was completed. The payment in wheat was received from the work supervisor on behalf of the project committee chairman, also the Union Parishad Chairman. The other seven maunds were kept by the supervisor. The women claimed their right to the outstanding seven maunds from the supervisor without result.

The local ward-member, who was nicknamed Budhu, meaning 'stupid', came by the work site and told the labourers that they would not receive the remaining seven maunds, as the site of the earthcutting had been changed. He claimed that by doing this the women had thereby broken the deal and that accordingly the payment would be reduced. At this, the women became furious and were close to beating him up with their baskets and spades. Budhu-member became nervous and fell on the ground with his motorbike. He was surrounded by the angry women, now far from silent, and obviously not intending to give up their claims. After they had spread him out on the ground, he promised to distribute the missing seven maunds. The following day this was done.

In another earthcutting scheme a number of the group members worked for two days without payment. The supervisor, who was selected by the project committee which was mainly comprised of Union Parishad people and was usually an effective tool of the local rich, explained that wheat was on its way and the women would receive their payment very soon. This went on for 20 days, creating difficulties for the women, who needed daily payment in order to feed their children. The group members, together with their co-ordination chairman Baherjan, sat down and had a serious discussion about the situation. Although they were working hard, they were unable to feed themselves and their families properly. After lengthy discussions they agreed to go to Manikgonj and put in a complaint at the District Commissioner's office and to tell the story to the local press, if no wheat was distributed the next day.

The following day the supervisor came back with the same old story about not being able to distribute any wheat. The group members, together with the rest of the labourers at the site, who were all female and numbered around 300, stopped work immediately and formed a big procession, then set out for Manikgonj District headquarters, 16 miles away. The people in the villages along the road had seen several processions, but never one with hundreds of women chanting slogans, demanding the salaries due to them and accusing the project committee of keeping their wheat.

When they reached the nearby market, not far from the work site, Baira Bazar, the Union Parishad Chairman happened to see the procession. He stopped it and got the situation clear after a talk with their leader, Baherjan, who was clever enough to understand the effect of the march to the DC and the leaking of the story to the local press. She accused the chairman of wrongfully withholding 20 days' payment and using the wheat for his own business. Confronted by the facts and 300 mobilized women, the chairman pulled off his shoes, gave them to Baherjan and asked her to humiliate him by beating him with them in public. This is a humiliating way to give an apology, a powerful symbol of contrition. The chairman was prepared to do anything to prevent the women from going to the DC with the complaint.

The women demanded immediate distribution of the wheat or the procession would continue. With this threat the chairman sent his men to Manikgonj to collect the wheat and the correct amount was distributed on that very day.

The women labourers started off for their villages with their fair share of wheat, lively women chanting slogans like 'Unity of poor women means strength' or 'Long live the unity of the poor'. *'Ekkota'* (unity), was heard all around. Collective mobilization for social justice pays off.

The daily wage

Diabari Gorib Bhumihin Samity, Diabari Poor Landless Society, in Harirampur *upazila*, Manikgonj District, with 33 group members, has been organized for two and a half years.

In the beginning a five-day Proshika training course on social analysis and organization-building was given, although this is not the usual way that Proshika operates. Two participants from this training course then started organizing the landless in their home village. When they discussed their main problems they found the low wage rate to be the major one. The *samity* was then formed.

Two years ago the day labourer rate in the high season was ten taka plus two meals. First the *samity* managed to raise it to 12 taka, later to 15 taka and during the last year up to 20 taka, plus two meals daily. The slack season rate has been raised from 7 to 15 taka.

On their initial attempt, they were boycotted by the landlords for two weeks. While they were without work they used their group savings to buy food. The boycott took place during peak harvesting time, when job opportunities are very good and the seasonal wage rate is at its highest, but they kept together, thereby developing deep trust and solidarity.

The group members now formed their general policy for contracts to perform agricultural work. The chairman, Khaleq, soon became the one that the landlords came to in order to ask the group members for their labour. He collects these demands and every evening the group sit together to allocate work among themselves for the next day. At every evening meeting the wage-money, which has been handed over by the landlords to the chairman, is evenly distributed among the members. Thus, a kind of labour-contracting society has emerged.

This group is also responsible for the landless of the locality who are not yet organized. All take part in the collective deals. This is a good example of further solidarity building. They stick very closely to the legal minimum wage.

The organized groups now cover six villages. They have formed a co-ordination committee consisting of three groups from these villages. Their collective and successful efforts of claiming the legal minimum wage rate has thereby spread throughout 18 villages, covering the whole locality.

Another aim is to maintain the 20 taka daily rate all year round, another is literacy. They are waiting until their organizing strength is strong enough before tackling more demanding tasks. There is a *khas* resource of 60 acres *bheel* (water-logged land) in the area. It is currently controlled illegally by means of fake documents by the landlords in collaboration with the local government officials. When the groups consider that they have gained the necessary organizational maturity, strength and numbers, they will start mobilizing for their legal right to the access of this *khas* resource. 'As we know the strength of our enemy, they have the money, the services from the government officials and the police, we have to be well prepared.' Having the *bheel* under their control would mean future substantial income from fishing and agriculture.

The group also plans to involve those who work in bonded labour in their aims. These people live in conditions close to slavery. They work only for big landlords on annual contracts with a yearly income of around 2500–3000 taka. Their daily work starts early in the morning, at 4 or 5 am, and continues up to ten at night or to midnight. Their work covers all areas. As agriculture is a year-round business and is labour intensive, there is rarely an idle hour. They take care of the cattle in the mornings, working in the fields during the day.

On some afternoons and evenings the labourers take products to the market place, carrying them on their heads, from a bamboo rod across their shoulders or by ox-cart. Then the cattle must be taken care of, before the day's work is over.

They are never free; not even during the most important annual Muslim holiday, Eid, are they unoccupied. Besides the yearly salary they have free housing and free food, which means a bench to sleep on or a bast-mat to roll out on the floor. They receive three meals a day: rice with the cheapest possible lentil soup (*keshuri*), not so long ago considered as cattle fodder, or rice together with seasonal vegetables in a curry. Every year they receive two *lungis*, two *gham*-

sas (neckerchiefs), two *genjis* (undershirts) and a *chador* (shawl) to wrap themselves in on cold winter nights. As a gift to Eid a secondhand shirt is usually distributed. There are, of course, a lot of cases where the conditions for bonded labourers are far worse than this.

They sell their labour in advance, their cash salary being paid when the year of contract is completed, but as they live away from their families, they have to take advantage from the cash salary to provide for their dependants' support, if it is accurate to talk in terms of provision of support. Sometimes they simply borrow money from the landlord, thereby becoming totally dependent on the *sahib*, who finds this one-tier dependency very useful. He can kick out his bonded labourers whenever he wishes.

The working week is three or four times longer than that of ordinary day labourers, with not a day free. In contrast, their payment is three or four times lower than that of the landless day labourers and there is no security.

There are hundreds of thousands of people living under these circumstances in rural Bangladesh and elsewhere. The day they decide to fight for the right to live as dignified human beings will be very important to the entire social system.

This is an example of organization with a sound ideological base. The groups are not only working for themselves, but for everyone of their class in the locality. This is important, not only for their improved economy, but also for their social interests.

Asha Nari Kalawan Samity (the Hope for the Women Welfare Society) was formed in late 1984 in Moharazpur village, in Mukshudpur *upazila*, Gopalgonj District. There are 18 members and their savings are five taka per month per member. They have regular weekly meetings. All the members live in the same *para* and all of them will take any kind of work in the village. All are landless and extremely poor, victims of the socio-economic system prevailing all over the country.

The chairman of the group, Rahela Khatun, and the cashier Hafeza Khatun were trained in human development and social analysis. After the training they had discussions with the rest of the members, all of whom were working on jute threshing during the harvesting period for the rich farmers of the village. The rate was fixed at one taka for threshing 20 bundles of jute. Between 8 am and 4 pm a woman can thresh at most 80 bundles, giving a daily wage of four taka. The women agreed that it was absurd to call this a full day's earning. The payment was one-seventh of the minimum wage for day labourers fixed by the government. They could not even buy one seer of wheat flour which cost 6.50 taka per seer. At the same time, the men's daily wage was 15 taka.

The members discussed their wage situation and decided that they would stop work till the rate for 20 bundles was raised to 2.50 taka. They also involved unorganized women in the locality, who agreed to their proposal to refuse work under such circumstances.

They put their proposal forward to the rich jute farmers, explaining their unity and firmness, but when the rich farmers refused to pay the new rate, the women immediately left for their homes. There was no jute threshing for a week.

The men stopped threshing as well, in support of the women's action. They all had wives, daughters, mothers or sisters and fully understood and agreed with the reasons for the action.

The jute farmers began to see their jute being destroyed, and they finally had to agree to the new rate. When they threatened to stop growing jute Rahela was quick to point out that they would no longer be rich if they left their fields barren.

They now earn ten taka per day instead of the previous four. By this action they have been able to start to change a system which for generations has made poor peoples' living conditions impossible. Only organized and united efforts among themselves can possibly lead them forward. In the next season they intend to raise the wage further, confident of the strength of their *samity*.

Equal pay for equal work

In Bahadurpur village, in Madaripur *upazila*, Madaripur District, Nari Mukti Samity (The Liberated Women's Society) was formed five years ago. The group consists of 14 women, all of them from marginal farmer families. They have monthly savings of five taka per member and hold meetings once a month. When needed, they have meetings more often. The area, which has a large population of Hindus, has a total of 20 organized women's groups and ten men's groups. They are all co-ordinated by a village co-ordination committee. Here, women are selling their labour for work in the fields, transplanting and weeding paddy.

Three years ago the women's groups had a number of discussions about the different rates of pay for women and men doing the same work in the fields. At that time the women received six taka daily, while the men were paid ten taka for exactly the same work. The rich farmers and the landlords preferred to hire women, not only because they cost less, but also because the women worked faster than the men.

The women group members claimed their right to the same pay for the same work, but the employers did not agree.

It was the season for IRRI cultivation. The fields were irrigated and ploughed and fully prepared for transplanting the paddy, so the village co-ordination committee decided to launch a strike. As most of the landless and the marginal farmers in the area were organized, no labourers were available for planting. The farmers and landlords were forced to agree on the equal pay claim to prevent their fields remaining barren.

Three years later, equal wages are still being paid and through united annual negotiations, the groups have succeeded in increasing the daily rate to 20 taka.

The marginal farmer group members began to think about further development of their organized strength. They were all experts in the work involved in IRRI cultivation, but because they were not able to irrigate their own tiny plots they sold their working skills only to the well-to-do farmers. They decided to pool their landholdings, and begin collective irrigation and farming. In order to obtain a loan from Proshika to purchase a diesel-power pump, they contacted their Proshika *kormi* and he made a feasibility study.

Four of the members had mortgaged their small landholdings so the group used 2000 taka from their savings and a loan of 9000 taka from Proshika to reclaim these plots, which amounted to 1.4 acres. Another 0.6 acre of the members' land was added, and their pooled acreage came to 2 acres. They then made an arrangement to provide the rich landholders with fields in the same area with irrigation facilities in return for one third of the crop as payment. This agreement of selling irrigation services amounted to 16 acres which, added to their 2 acres, brought the total to 18 acres.

With Proshika as guarantor they received a loan of 28757 taka from Bangladesh Krishi Bank for purchasing a low-lift diesel-power pump. To cover the first season's operation costs, they applied for another credit from Proshika of 20457 taka. Two women from the group were trained on how to manage the scheme at the Proshika ADC in Madaripur.

After the first season's harvest, they were able to repay the operation cost credit of 20457 taka, leaving a 10000 taka profit. In addition to this 42 maunds of paddy (1.55 tonnes) were distributed among the members, each of whom received three maunds (111kg, valued at approximately 500 taka). The power pump is an important element is this extremely profitable venture.

Income generation

Bidhoba Mohila Samity, the Widow Women Society, of Mustafapur village, in Madaripur District, has 16 members. They are all landless and have been organized for seven years. Their monthly savings are five taka per member. To start they had weekly meetings, then fortnightly, and now monthly meetings are held.

Nine months after the group had been formed, they decided to go into mat-making. They borrowed 1000 taka from Proshika to help buy raw materials together with to their own savings of about 500 taka. Raw materials had to be bought from far away, which meant high costs. After a month of production, they were able to repay the Proshika loan, but they gave up the project, as it proved to be unprofitable.

Later they went into rice husking instead. They put in their own savings, 900 taka, and took a new loan from Proshika of 2500 taka to purchase paddy in the market. They processed the paddy, which means boiling, drying and husking, and resold it in the market with a fairly good margin. There are two different kinds of paddy processing: the *atop*, which makes the white rice mainly used for cakes, sweets, pilau and biriani, which is only dried and husked; the other is *sidhaya*, the ordinary rice used everyday with curries, which is boiled, dried and husked before it is ready for consumption.

The paddy-processing project continued for three years. From the profits they leased a pond in the village, paying a total of 3000 taka for a five-year lease, to begin fish farming. The rice husking continued and the paddy left-overs from the husking process were used as fodder for the fish.

After two years of fish farming and paddy processing, they were able to use 8000 taka of their profits to pay off the mortgages of five group members. The released plots, totalling 1.5 acres, had been in the hands of rich villagers for years but could now be cultivated by the *samity* women. The income from jute, pulses and vegetables was shared on a fifty-fifty basis between the group and the plot owners.

The cultivation turned out to be profitable, mainly because the women themselves did all the work in the fields, hiring labour only for ploughing the land. This is a great achievement in an ordinary Bangladesh Muslim village.

In the first three years the income from the fish farming was 11,700 taka, which repaid not only the five mortgages but also the debt to Proshika.

The total income from all their activities over the five years until the expiry of the pond lease came to about 25 000 taka, by which time they were able to improve their diet by distributing fish from the pond to the group members every now and then. Each Eid a cash sum from the collective profits was also distributed among the members. After six years the final distribution amounted to 1500 taka each, including shares to three group members who had moved away from the village and to the family of one member who had died. The women used the money in different ways. One borrowed more and bought a second-hand rickshaw for 3200 taka. It is operated by her son and provides a daily income. Another bought six corrugated iron sheets for a permanent roof for her hut. The women who had their mortgaged land released now cultivate their plots themselves. The group has used their communal fund to buy paddy and jute at harvest time: this will be stored until it can be sold at higher rates. They are planning to start up a concrete slab making project as their next venture.

Ghasful Mohila Samity (The Flower of the Grass Women's Society) was formed three years ago in Baropaika village under Agailjhara *upazila* in Barisal district. It has 13 landless members, all outcast Hindus. They have weekly meetings and monthly savings of five taka per person. There is a total of three women's groups and three men's groups in the village.

None of the group members has any lands except their homesteads. They live in a remote area which is extensively flooded during the rainy season. Because job opportunities are rare, the women will take any kind of work in the fields on offer.

A year ago they obtained a loan of 3500 taka from Proshika to start a mat-making project. The input from their own savings was 1000 taka. The raw material for the mats, *hoogla* leaves, had to be obtained from a distant market place, so they asked members of the male groups to go and buy it for them.

All of the group take part in the mat-making, specializing in different stages of the production process. Upon completion the women themselves take the mats to the market. Usually the younger ones carry the mats to the market and the elderly women do the selling. They go to sell their products twice every week at the local market place three miles away from their village.

In one week, they have to procure 5–600 taka's worth of raw material to cover their needs. Each mat costs around 6–7 taka to make and is sold for 10–12 taka. They produce an average of 10 mats per day, 70 mats per week. The weekly profit is around 280 taka which, after expenses, gives a total profit of just above 1000 taka per month. They have repaid the Proshika loan, and the group members get a daily wage. The rest of the profit is kept by the *samity* to be distributed as a lump sum once every year.

Their main problem is the distance to the market, where they buy the *hoogla* leaves. These have been conveyed by boat to the village, demanding some additional expenditures.

Although the income from this project is very limited, it is very important to the group member's economy. There are few possibilities of any cash income for women in this isolated locality and the women are proud of their contribution to the family income.

In the village Kulappadi in Madaripur *upazila*, Madaripur District, Sonali Mohila Samity, the Golden Women's Society, was formed three years ago. The group consists of 22 members, who have savings of five taka per person monthly and bi-monthly meetings. There are a total of six men's and three women's groups in the village.

A year ago this particular *samity* took a lease on a pond situated within the village. The lease was for 12 years and the tank was owned by a marginal farmer of the locality. The pond was in bad shape and had not been used for several years. They got a loan of 11 000 taka from Proshika for re-excavation and fish farming and put in 3000 taka of their own savings.

As the monsoon arrived early, they could not fully complete the re-excavation, and 2000 taka was left unused. The re-excavation was done partly by the group members themselves and partly by hired labourers. When the re-excavation was finally completed, the dimensions of the pond were 100ft wide by 60ft long and 6ft deep.

During the first season they caught fish worth 4500 taka. They had developed their own fish nursery, and were able to sell fish fry to wholesalers even in the first year, after supplying their own needs.

The loan from Proshika will be repaid within three years, with nine years of the lease still to run, while the profits remain untouched by the group.

The women manage everything themselves except the marketing of the fish. For that purpose, male group members from the village take the catch to Madaripur market. Fish food consists of the leftovers from rice husking, compost and oil-cakes.

The 12-year lease should make this fish farm a profitable venture. As there was no conflict over the pond and the lease term was for such a long period of time, the investment in re-excavation was worthwhile. The women are confident, knowing that the annual income will increase. They are managing on their own and looking forward to incomes from the pond for many years to come.

Popular theatre for mobilization

Popular theatre has been developed into a widely utilized and efficient tool for the exposure of social issues and the patterns of exploitation and power structure of rural Bangladesh. Organized groups themselves plan and stage the dramas. They have themselves experienced what they want to reveal to others. The combination of the direct participation of the organized and the high entertainment value of what is known as consciousness-raising through critical dramas has paved the way for its extreme popularity and efficacy.

One of the areas where popular theatre has been successfully used and developed is in Nagarpur in Tangail District. Shova Rani Mondal, a female fieldworker from Nagarpur ADC, described how the popular theatre can be a tool in the struggle of the organized groups.

In 1984–5 a very large road-constructing project under the Food for Work programme was being carried out in Badra Union. Group members of some 60–65 Proshika-organized groups were involved in the scheme. Of these, 35 groups had Shova as their *kurmi*; 17 were women's *samitys*. The age of these groups varied between one and six years. It was part of Shova's daily routine to come to the worksite for formal talks about problems with the group members or for discussions and meetings when needed.

The most common problems of the group members were:

- irregular payment;
- inaccurate measurement of the work they had performed;
- that women labourers were 'disencouraged' to get work by the Project Committee;
- women labourers were often cheated of their fair payment.

In every scheme like this there has to be a noticeboard at the worksite, giving the basic facts about the project and about the rate of payment. In this case it was that 1000 cubic feet of earth moved from the road-side pits would be rewarded with 50 seers of wheat, the same basic payment as elsewhere. Shova and the group members discovered that the measurements were always taken from non-organized working groups. These were close to the supervisor of the project, and were rewarded for sanctioning his cheating. They received 40 seers while the organized groups received only 30–35 seers, but all groups were cheated: none received the 50 seers they were entitled to, a typical form of misappropriation in this kind of scheme.

These points were raised in the daily discussions among the group members at the worksite. They all became well aware of the cheating and decided to take united action against it.

They demanded a noticeboard with information about the payment rate at the worksite. The Union Parishad Chairman, who was also chairman of the project committee, asked them where they had learned about such a board. Some of the group members explained that they had been to training in Manikgonj and visited another scheme, where there was a signboard stating the rate of payment of 50 seers per 1000 cubic feet. They then asked whether the payment should not be the same all over Bangladesh? The chairman was unhappy about this development among the labourers and began to discourage Shova visiting for regular meetings and discussions with the workers.

The women group members mobilized. Fifteen hundred women labourers organized a procession, chanting slogans demanding 'regular payment, fair payment, fair measurement' and that the payment should not be made on the big weekly market day. The procession headed towards the Agarpur *upazila* headquarters. The chairman, knowing what the consequences would be if his misappropriation was disclosed, became uneasy and tried to meet with Shova to try to negotiate to stop the procession but she claimed that she had urgent work to attend to in another place. The chairman was forced to confront the demonstrators, but they were not interested in his proposals. They assured him then if he didn't move they would 'help' him to get out their way. He fled and the procession continued to Nagarpur.

When they reached the *upazila* headquarters the UNO was astounded to see this huge gathering of mobilized women demanding to know why there was no noticeboard at their worksite and why they were given unfair payment. They also accused the UNO of being the main culprit in the misappropriation because he knew about it but did nothing.

The UNO, faced with facts and a militant movement, promised immediate action. A committee was formed on the spot consisting of the chairman, some labourer representatives and the Proshika *kurmi*. While the procession waited, the committee came to an agreement. Fresh measurements were to be taken from the start of the scheme and the payment of 50 seers per 1000 cubic feet would be paid retrospectively to all labour teams working at the site, meeting all the demands of the demonstrating labourers.

The chairman then tried a new tack. To avoid the organized local labourers, who were difficult to deal with, he recruited fresh labourers. With unorganized workers he counted on being able to get into profitable cheating again, but the groups told the new workers about their previous actions against the chairman and, once they understood, there was no work done for two weeks. Then the chairman was notified that technicians from CARE were expected to come and check on the progress of the construction work. Immediately he asked the organized group members to begin work again.

The group members gained courage from their victory and wanted to show the story of their mobilization to other landless people in the locality to demonstrate that it is possible to win against the élite. They decided to stage a popular theatre on the theme of their recent experiences.

There were 3000 people in the audience, not only poor villagers but also local well-to-do people. The drama, *natok*, was performed by the group members themselves without a prepared script or dialogue. They told the history of the mobilization from the first steps of initial informal discussions about common problems to the successful mobilization for fair payment and against misappropriation. The serious social issues were treated in an entertaining manner and the audience was very enthusiastic, but there were some less happy faces among those in the audience belonging to the local élite.

The impact of the drama was clear. Key points from the dialogue could be heard in the bazaar or at tea stalls for many days to come and some of the phrases became popular sayings from then on. This showed it to be a tremendous success as a popular drama. It appealed to the ordinary villagers' thinking and *chinta* (concern) and was representative of their own humour and culture.

There was a further episode in the story. The chairman, whose actions had been fully disclosed in the drama, picked out Shova, the female Proshika worker, as being mainly responsible for this criticism. She then became the target of his revenge.

A story was fabricated by the chairman and his companions. When a simple thief was caught in the bazaar the chairman offered to drop his prosecution if he co-operated with him. He was instructed to make a speech in the bazaar to the effect that he was an old criminal friend of Shova's brother with whom he had committed a number of thefts together over the last five years and and that Shova was part of their gang. As a Proshika *kurmi*, she could move around in the villages freely, then tell her brother and his companions which houses it would be good to burgle. After the speech the chairman sent two of his men to arrest Shova and her brother. She refused to ride on their motorbikes, but came later in a rickshaw.

The thief then repeated his story again, parrot-fashion. Shova and her brother were publicly accused of being responsible for these criminal activities. Shova asked if she was allowed to defend herself against these allegations in public. She then put some questions to the thief. 'You have been co-operating with my brother for five years, met him more or less every day?' 'Yes', answered the thief. 'Then tell his name,' Shova continued. The thief was unable to answer.

At this point a local policeman turned up to interrogate the thief and it soon became obvious to the people assembled that there was something strange about his story and that it had been fabricated by the chairman as his revenge against Shova for her part in making his misappropriations public. Even one of the men who had been sent to arrest Shova, understanding that he had been cheated, openly protested against the allegations and defended Shova and her brother.

Since it was getting late, Shova asked the chairman if he intended to send them to the police station or if they could go home. As his story had been proved false he asked them to go home, but told them that they were to attend his chambers, when he required.

Later, while Shova was performing her ordinary Proshika duties, she was stopped now and then by another police officer who had been asked to lean on her until she left the Proshika job. The chairman obviously hoped that his uniform would put pressure on her. She replied that her job was none of his business.

The officer in charge of the Nagarpur *thana* also showed a keen interest in Shova. His proposals were more personal as he asked her to follow him into his private quarters many a time. There seemed to be a number of problems of different kinds for a female fieldworker, trying to work in the interest of the organized rural poor.

A regular week-long programme on popular theatre was held at the Proshika ADC in Nagarpur at that time. On the final day a drama was staged to which all *upazila* officials, along with the police and the local élite, were invited. Altogether about 6000 spectators assembled to see the performance.

The drama had been updated to include more recent events, including the chairman's fabricated story and the immoral behaviour of the police officer-in-charge.

The quality of the drama was very high and the audience was amazed that the actors could manage without any rehearsal or script. Also, because it was drama in an efficient mirror of the actions of the elite in the popular and humorous style typical of the people's theatre it made the spectators recognize the nature of the elite, focusing on the well-known local characters. This form of critical social drama is more efficient than a hundred speeches or thousands of pamphlets.

Since the drama was staged there has been no harassment whatsoever from any quarters against Shova or the Proshika work in general in the area. The élite know that their misdoings will be exposed in dramas which reach thousands of people. Popular theatre has become a tool in the struggle for social justice in the hands of the organized.

Organizational strength — the way forward

Khorshed Alum belongs to Nabajagaran Bhumihin Samity (the Newly Awakened Landless Society). The group has 18 members and was formed five years ago in the village of Paishana, Nagarpur *upazila*, Tangail District. There are together seven men's and two women's groups in the village, which means that all of the landless are organized.

Four years ago Khorshed Alum went for social consciousness and human development training through Proshika. He has often played a vital role as a spokesman for the landless and is an outspoken speaker at annual general gatherings of the organized and a leading voice when mobilizing for wage increases, conducting negotiations with landlords or ensuring the correct amount of wheat at Food for Work schemes.

There are 410 organized groups in the area, distributed in Nagarpur, Deldoar and Daulatpur *upazilas*. All these groups are co-ordinated by Bhumi Sramik Shomonoy Committee (the Land Labourers' Co-ordination Committee) which consists of 71 members from the 410 groups. As chairman of this committee, Khorshed Alum is the holder of a very responsible and at times uncomfortable position. His views are expressed in the following interview.

Please tell about the organization of your area.

The 71 members of the Co-ordination Committee are the representatives from the Union Co-ordination Committees. Out of the total 15 are women and 56 are men. We hold our meetings on the thirtieth of each month at the Proshika centre in Nagarpur. When necessary, we include Proshika *kurmis* in the meetings, but generally they do not take part.

What is the percentage of attendance of the members of the committee?

Usually almost all are present. Sometimes two or three are missing, but just as often a couple of interested group members also attend the meetings. They are welcome. On average we have a 98 per cent attendance. If a union representative fails to come, any group member of that union can attend.

Why has it been important to form this greater Co-ordination Committee?

Well, you see, when we realized that organizing has to be our own work and the Proshika workers only can help us, we had to do it ourselves. Our own co-ordination also has to be done by us. We have to get to know each other and further develop contacts and co-ordinated action between the groups. This makes the organization stronger; through this a group is never alone. It is the necessary cement for the building of a *pucca* organizational structure. Today we have achieved this. There are some groups 16–17 miles away from Nagarpur. Without co-ordination, they would be left outside. All groups have to be part of a greater entity, none is allowed to get isolated. The benefits of co-ordination are recognized by all the group members. The co-ordination committee is virtually a mirror of the whole working area.

What are the main points of discussion at the monthly meetings of the Co-ordination Committee?

Whatever problems and issues arise. We discuss and decide what steps will be taken, how to reform groups that have become inactive or views on the working pattern of the Proshika *kurmis*. Let me give an example. At the last meeting we were discussing our number of groups. It is always easy to strive for a rapid increase in the number of organized groups. You can even boast about how many you are, but as the discussion went on, more and more emphasis was put on the quality of the groups. It is more important that the groups are developing social awareness than to create hundreds of groups with only a feeble knowledge of what it is all about. Quality stands before quantity.

How would you evaluate the savings and income-generating activities of the groups?

Savings and income-generating activities are not the main objectives of the groups. They merely provide minor security within our class, to break our dependency on the local money-lender or landlord.

Initially, the savings and economic activities are important for the basic group forming. This paves the way for mobilization later on and, more importantly, it helps the landless to become active instead of passive, to bring them together as a class. Economic activities must never be taken as the main objective for the groups. The main objective is something very different.

What is the main objective?

The main objective is to change the social system. For this we have discussions, we receive training, we have workshops. Unless and until the vast majority of the people in our society benefit, no development is ever possible. The rich and the poor can never live happily together. Thorough change is essential. As long as we do not want change or do not work for change, there will not be any change. The transformation of the present social system is our main objective and goal.

How is this change in the social system possible?

As long as the broad majority of the people do not understand the methods and extent of exploitation, there will be no change. The poor as a class have to become socially conscious, grasping the real relations between exploiters and exploited. Poor people have to be awakened from their sleep. They have to become more vocal. Only a continuous process will achieve this. We can never limit our thinking only to our area. Even if we become extremely strong locally, if we mobilize on a broad and militant base over a wider area within a year or two, it will not be the solution. Only a nationwide movement can secure the thorough social change needed. That will take some time, but the seed of destruction of the rich is hidden in our struggle for existence.

What is your opinion regarding the government's development activities, for example the construction of roads, schools and hospitals?

You see, the roads, culverts, bridges and what-not are not for us: they merely exist in our society. There are hospitals, there are schools, but I cannot send my children to these schools, my wife is refused treatment as these hospitals. These development activities serve only the rich, and all the construction activities do is to create a new generation of rich traders and contractors. Not long ago we only had one brick-field in this area, now there are plenty. The number of cement traders has increased ten-fold over a couple of years, but only a limited number of people is becoming rich, investing in buses and becoming large-scale rickshaw owners. It is only benefiting the rich.

In these so-called development activities, I would say 85 per cent of the people are not involved either directly or indirectly. The government may call it development, but as so few benefit from our point of view, I cannot consider it as such.

What is your view regarding the claiming of khas *land and the increase of wages?*

The mobilization to claim *khas* land and increase wages, and the successes of these attempts, are only limited gains because they give financial benefit only to a small section of people in a particular area. To change the social system these actions are not sufficient, but these efforts and successes are, of course, not without value: they give a direction to our movement against the rich to change the social structure. If our mobilization is limited to these kinds of actions, then our main objective will be left out.

What active part can the greater organization play in this?

Proshika is a development organization. Their fieldworkers are paid by Proshika. They can't go beyond their own limits. They are not landless. They are only working to promote the landless' organization-building. Proshika has its limits. As an NGO it has to obey the rules and regulations of the government. Their workers also have to work within these limits. However our Co-ordination Committee is a representative body of the organized landless, and does not have limitations like that. Our objective is to change the social system. Our strength, or lack of strength, is our only limitation. At the point where Proshika *kurmis* have to stop their work, we start. For this reason, we do not generally have the *kurmis* at our Co-ordination Committee meetings.

Could you finally cite one or two examples of group mobilization?

There are so many cases. One of them is a Food for Work scheme. During the monsoon 50 maunds of wheat were allocated for the repair work of a primary school. The group which was to do the work pressurized the Union Parishad Chairman to give them the total allocation. First he refused, as it would mean that he would lose all possibility of some extra income, but he was compelled. The group members formed a team and completed the work, earning praise from the local people. When the work was properly completed, all the group members went with the master-roll to the UNO office, but the head assistant refused to accept the master-roll without first getting his share. He didn't care whether the work that had been executed was good or bad, his only concern was his share of the allotment. We pretended to be fools, asking him what he meant by talking about a share for him. There were 50 maunds allotted for the work, but nothing was mentioned about a share to him. We proceeded to the UNO, asking him to change his head assistant's mind and behaviour or we would throw him out of the upstairs window. The UNO was irritated at this, asking us to respect government officials. We asked how uneducated village people could learn good behaviour, when we faced this kind of treatment from a government official. The UNO made the head assistant take care of the master-roll.

Khorshed Alum is one of those rural landless, often branded as uneducated, ignorant and simple-minded village people. He is very clear and firm in his speech, with a consciousness and an ability to sort information and form arguments that too many of those who call themselves educated lack. If only there were more people like Khorshed Alum in rural Bangladesh.